ASPERGER SYNDROME

AND ADOLESCENCE

FAIR WINDS
PRESS

GLOUCESTER, MASSACHUSETTS

First published in the USA in 2001 by
Fair Winds Press
33 Commercial Street
Gloucester, MA 01930

10 9 8 7 6 5 4 3 2 1

Printed and bound in Canada

Cover design by
Laura Shaw Design

Book design by
SYP Design & Production, Inc.
www.sypdesign.com

ISBN 1-931412-69-3

*The information in this book is for educa-
tional purposes only. It is not intended to
replace the advice of a professional counselor.*

ASPERGER SYNDROME

AND ADOLESCENCE

Helping Preteens

and Teens

Get Ready for the

Real World

TERESA BOLICK, PH.D.

To my son, Seth
And to all "my kids"

Acknowledgments

The ideas shared in this book represent the experiences of scores of children, adolescents, and families. Without their willingness to tell their stories, there would have been no ideas to share. Thank you all.

I must also thank the professionals—teachers, speech/language pathologists, occupational therapists, physical therapists, psychotherapists, physicians, and fellow psychologists—who have brainstormed with me over the years. All of those hours of "Well, what if we try…" will not be forgotten. Whether you taught "my kids" or me, you taught in the most profound sense of the word.

My editor, Holly Schmidt, has been a trooper. I still can't imagine what possessed Holly to take a chance on a psychologist who had lots of stories but little else to prove that she could write a book. But, I'm glad that she took that chance!

Over the years, my family and friends have provided unflagging support for virtually any endeavor I attempted. Over the last several months, their patience for being neglected and their willingness to keep "feeding" me anyway have been truly remarkable. Thank you all—especially you, Dad.

And to my husband and son, Stephen and Seth Taylor…there are no words to express completely what you have given me. Your encouragement and patience are indispensable. Your love has fueled my efforts. And, most of all, you have reminded me daily about our journeys in the real world.

Table of Contents

Introduction

This book is about journeys. Over the years, I have had the privilege of working with children, adolescents, and adults with Asperger Syndrome (AS). In fact, I knew some of them before I knew about Hans Asperger and AS. This book would not have been possible without the generosity of all of these individuals and their families. As they shared their journeys with me, they also revealed their experience and wisdom. It is their experience and wisdom that I want to share with you, the reader.

This book is also about partnerships—between parent and adolescent, between parents, among family members, between professional and adolescent, and between professionals and parents. One lesson I've learned is that none of us should be forced to travel alone.

This book is not intended to be the definitive resource on Asperger Syndrome. Other authors have served that purpose more eloquently and completely than I ever could. (*Asperger Syndrome*, edited by Ami Klin, Fred R. Volkmar, and Sara S. Sparrow, and *Asperger's Syndrome* by Tony Attwood are examples of comprehensive and remarkably detailed references.) Instead, the current book is an effort to bring to life the experience of being an adolescent first and, secondarily, an adolescent with AS. As you read, you may recognize not only the stories, but also the feelings of being young and perplexed.

This book is written for parents. Many of you knew all along that something was different about your child, even when professionals said otherwise. Others among you struggled with diagnoses that didn't quite fit. Some of you had to endure the criticism of concerned family and friends, those who suggested that your child would be "fine" if you just changed your parenting style. All the while, you had to manage the tantrums that came when the seams in the socks weren't right or when you let the peas touch the rice on the dinner plate. You worried late at night about whether she would ever be invited to a birthday party—and about how she could possibly "behave herself" if she did go. You served as organizers of homework and countless school projects and as "naggers" for showers, washed hair, and brushed teeth. This book strives to offer you strategies, some old and some new, that have worked for others. This book strives to remind you that no matter what, you don't have to take AS personally.

This book is written in part for teachers and other professionals. Especially at the middle and high school levels, it is hard to find time to get to know all of the students who pass through your door. The student who has a wealth of information, but a lack of organization and follow-through can be frustrating. Why won't he just show what he knows? The adolescent girl who has the vocabulary of a professor but the social skills of a preschooler can be maddening. Doesn't she know about respect for authority? Students with AS require extra effort—to understand them, to teach them, and to keep from taking their behavior personally. This book strives to provide tips for the teacher or therapist who is "in the trenches."

To the adolescent or young adult with Asperger Syndrome, this book seeks to celebrate your gifts and to help you find ways around your glitches. Donna Williams commented in *Sombody Somewhere,* "I didn't want to change my personality. I had had enough cosmetic surgery performed upon my personality. I simply wanted to know what pieces or concepts I was missing that stopped me from being able to change my own behavior and use my own resources." This book is about explaining "rules" and concepts and providing strategies so that you can use your own resources. The strategies may seem no better than the ones you already use. They are offered in the hopes of giving you a choice about how to make your journey through life.

CHAPTER ONE

Journeys and Partnerships

Sally's ninth grade health class had been studying the food chain for a few weeks. They learned about herbivores, carnivores, and omnivores. They learned about the balance of nature and the importance of food sources for all living things.

One question on the chapter test was, "Imagine that you are at the top of the food chain. Give an example of a meal that would make you a primary consumer of meat and a secondary consumer of plant matter."

Sally wrote, "Whoa, dude! i am a VEGETAIRIAN! i NEVER touch meat!" When a second question referred to being a carnivore, Sally again took offense: "Duh. What didn't you get before? i am a VEGETAIRIAN!"

Sally's teacher was concerned about more than her use of capitals and correct spelling. The teacher wrote a comment on the paper, "You don't have to be disrespectful. You can imagine the situation and answer the question."

Sally's parents knew that she wasn't being disrespectful. Sally just didn't know how to take a perspective other than her own.

Although Hans Asperger only wrote about boys, he would have recognized Sally. In fact, many parents of boys and girls will recognize Sally's unique approach to everyday life. Sally's difficulties with abstract language, with using her imagination, and with taking another point of view are some of the characteristics that we now associate with Asperger Syndrome (AS).

Sally and her parents had shared a roller-coaster journey through life. Her humor and creativity had brought them exciting adventures. Her social awkwardness had sometimes left them confused and discouraged. But, through the "dangerous curves" and peaks and valleys of their journey, they managed a "working partnership" that sustained them.

Adolescence is a challenging journey for all families. For families of adolescents with AS, though, the challenge can be even more intense. Everybody makes it through, but the whole process is a lot easier if people can work together.

WHAT IS ASPERGER SYNDROME? A QUICK REVIEW

WHAT THE EXPERTS SAY

The definition of AS has been revised and re-revised over the last sixty years. In the *Diagnostic and Statistical Manual of Mental Disorders* (Fourth edition, text revision, 2000), the American Psychiatric Association (APA) lists the following diagnostic criteria for "Asperger's Disorder":

o Qualitative impairment in social interaction, such as marked impairment in the use of nonverbal behavior, failure to develop developmentally appropriate peer relationships, lack of spontaneous joint attention with others, or lack of social reciprocity
o Restricted repetitive and stereotyped patterns of behavior and interests, such as intense and narrow preoccupation with certain topics or routines, inflexible adherence to routines, repetitive motor mannerisms, or preoccupation with parts of objects
o Clinically significant impairment in daily role functioning
o No "clinically significant" delay in language
o No "clinically significant" delay in cognitive development or self-help skills

○ Failure to meet criteria for another specific Pervasive Developmental Disorder or Schizophrenia.

This list is likely to change yet again as researchers and clinicians prepare for the next revision of the DSM. In the meantime, diagnosis of AS continues to depend in part on "scientific" criteria and in large part on clinical intuition.

A PRACTICAL DEFINITION

As we consider the journey through adolescence, it makes sense to have a practical view of AS. For our purposes, AS means:

○ Awkwardness in communication, despite strong vocabulary and grammar
○ Difficulty in "reading" the behavior of others
○ A preference for predictability
○ A tendency toward specific and intense interests
○ (Sometimes) inefficient organization and productivity, despite strong intellectual abilities
○ (Sometimes) challenges in integrating sensory information
○ (Often) clumsiness
○ (Sometimes) problems in regulating anxiety or mood

If we look at AS through a different lens, though, we can reframe some of these "deficits" as assets. Because an individual with AS is unfettered by the chains of social convention or "manners," he may be able to identify unique solutions that no one else notices. "Unfettered" thinking can also lead to remarkable creativity in the arts. A lack of preoccupation with the social politics of life may also allow the individual with AS to devote herself to dogged pursuit of answers to complex questions. A preference for predictability and rules can also lead one to be a model student or employee—working hard to meet expectations, responding honestly, and doing "a day's work for a day's pay." Perhaps most importantly, individuals with AS help the rest of us stay honest and grounded. In considering their questions and comments, we can reflect upon why we do the things we do, why the Western world is so filled with contradictions, and why we all can benefit from a partner (at least every once in a while).

WHAT CAUSES ASPERGER SYNDROME?

It is still hard to answer this question. Past inconsistency in the diagnostic guidelines has made it difficult to know who fits in which category and to pinpoint the causes of AS. Better diagnosis and research on the causes of autism have given us some promising leads, though.

Although we don't have all of the answers to why it happens, it is becoming more clear that the idiosyncrasies of AS are rooted in developmental differences in the brain and nervous system. Our understanding of the specifics of inefficient brain functioning in AS is in its infancy. One thing is quite clear, however: AS is not a result of a single, or even a few, "glitches." Instead, it represents difficulties in the various structures and pathways that allow us to perceive, understand, and respond to information from multiple sources at the same time. Social communication and relationships probably represent the ultimate challenge to these nervous system processes!

Finally, research and clinical observation now allow us to say with some conviction that Asperger Syndrome, autism, and related social communication difficulties are **neurodevelopmental disorders.** In other words, they are associated with inefficiencies in the brain and nervous system. They are present across the lifespan, probably beginning before birth. They represent differences in development, not just delays. Perhaps most importantly for parents, we now know that these challenges are not simply a result of "spoiling" or poor parenting.

LESSONS FROM PARENTS, TEACHERS, PEERS, AND PEOPLE WITH AS

Many of the most helpful ideas about AS have come from the folks who live with it every day. Parents may describe their child by saying, "He's smart, but he doesn't get it." Teachers ask, "How can she know so much and not be able to apply the information?" Peers or siblings charge, "Boy, is he clueless!" Liane Holliday Willey, both a parent of a child with AS and an individual with AS herself, wrote most eloquently in *Pretending to Be Normal*, "Small group conversations make my nerves feel like they are wearing stilts on an icy pavement."

As a clinical psychologist, I have learned many lessons about AS from the children, adolescents, and adults with whom I work. Again and again, they and their families give me this message: "My brain and nervous system allow me to do well in many aspects of life. But sometimes I interact without understanding. I am often overwhelmed by the information that floods my body and mind. I may choose unusual ways of coping, but these help me manage. I may seem rigid, but I'm doing the best I can to be flexible. In spite of my quirks, I am trying to get to the same place as everyone else. I just take a different, and sometimes slower, path."

SO, WHAT DOES ADOLESCENCE HAVE TO DO WITH IT?

"It was the best of times, it was the worst of times..."
—Charles Dickens, *A Tale of Two Cities*

Most of us remember adolescence as vividly as any other time in our lives. Adolescence spans our "preteen" and "teenage" years. During those years, many of us are acutely aware of ourselves. We worry about how we look, what we do and how we do it, who our friends are, and (eventually) what we're going to do when we "grow up." We struggle with how independent we really are. We begin to think for ourselves (or at least we think we do).

Fortunately, developmental change during puberty supports the adolescent's push for more independence in everyday life. While we often focus on the physical and hormonal changes of adolescence, the most dramatic changes are invisible to the naked eye. The brain and nervous system change dramatically during adolescence. New brain pathways are created. Unnecessary connections are "pruned." All told, brain and nervous system development during these years allows the adolescent to think more abstractly and more efficiently. In addition, the increased ability to think abstractly supports the adolescent's quest for social and emotional meaning.

Our culture expects a lot from adolescents. These increased expectations for adolescents probably weren't driven by specific knowledge of the fantastic brain development that occurs during puberty. It is more likely that our culture and schools based their expectations upon observation of what children could do at different ages. For a moment, though, ponder these questions: Why do we teach algebra in eighth or ninth grade, rather than in fourth? Why don't we teach philosophy to third graders? Why do we feel comfortable with a fourteen-year-old babysitter, but not with an eleven-year-old? Why can eighteen-year-olds vote, while sixteen-year-olds can't? During times of war, why does the United States government draft nineteen-year-olds, but not younger adolescents? The answers to these questions don't reflect simply the fact that older adolescents know more. The answers reflect our assumption that older adolescents think differently. They are able to integrate their thoughts and feelings in a way that makes them wiser and more responsible. The changes that occur over the course of adolescence, then, are probably a combination of brain and nervous system development and the experiences we provide for children during these years.

WHAT HAPPENS TO THE ADOLESCENT WITH ASPERGER SYNDROME?

SOCIAL COMMUNICATION CHALLENGES

Many of the challenges of typical adolescent development strike at the heart of the inefficiencies of children with neurodevelopmental disorders such as AS. Regardless of specific diagnosis, most children with neurodevelopmental disorders are inefficient in pragmatic and social communication. They interpret what was said, not what was meant. They have trouble adjusting their own verbal and nonverbal communication to the situation. At an age when success depends on both "walking the walk" and "talking the talk," adolescents with AS are at a distinct disadvantage.

Difficulties in social communication and differences in brain functioning can also interfere with the child's social awareness and ability to take another person's point of view. Reading between the lines, knowing the unspoken rules, and telling "little white lies" are challenging concepts and skills. Concepts such as modesty and discretion are even more perplexing. Yet, during adolescence, one's ability to fit in depends more and more upon these skills.

One mother told the story of thirteen-year-old Jamie's first meeting with her cousin's boyfriend. As the sixteen-year-old cousin introduced her boyfriend, Jamie looked closely at the young man. When it was her turn to greet him, Jamie blurted out, "Your face is covered with acne!"

While most thirteen-year-old girls would have noticed the young man's unfortunate case of acne, most would also have avoided comment. Even after the cousin and her boyfriend left, Jamie was unable to understand her mother's admonition against such remarks. "But, Mom," she said, "He does have acne. You always tell me not to lie."

SENSORIMOTOR AND REGULATORY CHALLENGES

At a time when most adolescents are acutely aware of themselves and their bodies, youngsters with AS are often still struggling with sensorimotor challenges (for example, Where is my body in space? How fast can I move? How much pressure can I exert? How can I stand that awful noise?). They are still getting used to the body they have always had; thus, this new body that changes virtually every day is particularly confusing. For the adolescent whose AS is associated with clumsiness, sports and physical education classes can be setups for failure and/or teasing. In a culture where how you move is almost as important as how you look, physical awkwardness can be a very real source of emotional pain. Sensory and regulatory difficulties also become harder to manage. Comfortable sweat pants and old flannel shirts are less acceptable in middle school than they were in the elementary grades. The "soothing rituals" that were accepted (or overlooked) in childhood can lead to ridicule or criticism in adolescence. Not only are the soothing strategies less welcome, but the demands for sensorimotor control are more intense!

MENTAL MAPS

Adolescence is a time of "finding oneself" (at least a version of oneself). In adolescence, few find themselves, but they do begin the quest. Casting off old values (usually those of their parents!) and finding new values and opinions require thinking, feeling, comparing, and sharing with peers. The cognitive and communicative challenges associated with AS can hamper this discovery process. Thus, the adolescent with AS may be left without a "mental map" of himself or herself.

Adolescence is also a time of learning new skills for regulating emotion. The adolescent with AS may still be struggling to manage the primary emotions (happiness, sadness, anger, and fear). As new feelings and sensations flood the nervous system, the adolescent with AS is understandably baffled. Complex feelings (such as guilt or embarrassment) and sexual feelings are virtually impossible to manage with a strict "right vs. wrong" rule-bound approach. Yet adolescents with AS often are still relying on "the rules." Even if the rules don't always apply, they often represent the best way to manage the "map" of the journey from here to there.

MANAGING BEHAVIOR

Nowhere is the rule-bound approach more inefficient than in the regulation of adolescent behavior. Even the most logical rule (for example, "don't swear") becomes fraught with pitfalls. Rules that work to regulate the behavior of an adolescent with AS can backfire when he quotes them to the 200-pound eighth grader on the bus! Rules that govern physical display and sexual behavior come into question when virtually every movie and TV show includes bare skin and sexy behavior. No wonder Donna Williams, an adult with autism, wrote: "What I wanted . . . were rules I could carry around with me that applied to all situations, regardless of context. I wanted rules without exceptions."

PROBLEM SOLVING AND DECISION MAKING

The self-regulatory and coping strategies used by most adolescents depend upon complex cognitive processes. They think about events and the associated feelings. They brainstorm about how the current situation matches past experiences. But many adolescents with AS struggle with complex cognitive processing or problem solving. Thus, it is difficult for them to hold onto the facts of the situation and mentally test possible solutions. The task of testing possible solutions becomes particularly taxing when the answers don't conform to one of "the rules." These inefficiencies can affect social, emotional, and academic situations in many aspects of daily life.

Eighteen-year-old Sam was about to take his driver's license road test for the fourth time. He was quite anxious, as he had failed so many times before. As we talked about his anxiety, he asked if he could ask a "silly" question. "What should I do if the light turns red when I'm in the middle of the intersection?" Although my experience with Massachusetts drivers tempted me to make a flip remark, I restrained myself and talked with Sam about all of the possible solutions. Then I said, "But, Sam, stop-lights always turn yellow before they turn red." "So?" Sam replied. "You can stop on yellow, you know," I suggested. Sam replied, "You can? I always learned that green means go and red means stop and yellow means caution. Nobody taught me that you can stop on yellow."

Imagine what complex decision making is like if you have trouble inferring that you can stop on a yellow light. It was little wonder that Sam was completely befuddled by topics like how to know if a girl liked him!

By the way, Sam did get his license. He not only became a competent driver but also an amazingly safe driver. He conscientiously obeyed traffic laws, paid his car insurance bills on time, and changed his oil every 3000 miles!

PLANNING AND ORGANIZATION

Adolescent life requires planning and organization. Whether at school or at home, the adolescent with AS is likely to face increased expectations for "responsibility," "independence," "respect," and "inhibition." Schoolwork no longer consists mainly of worksheets and fill-in-the-blank questions. Reading assignments require "reaction papers," not just recall of the plot and names of the main characters. Asperger Syndrome, like most neurodevelopmental disorders, can produce "glitches" in the executive functions that facilitate planning, organization, and initiation of goal-directed behavior. The adolescent with AS literally may not know where or how to start. Inefficiencies in inhibiting automatic or habitual responses make it hard for him/her to keep to the topic or task at hand. And if he/she manages to start and keep on track, stopping (knowing when the task is completed) can be a problem.

Sixteen-year-old Lorraine came into the office looking pale and exhausted. When asked about her tiredness, she explained that she had been up until 3 a.m. the night before, working on a paper for history. "I didn't get started til midnight because I couldn't decide what to write about," she began. "I was only supposed to write two pages," she said. "But, I just couldn't figure out what to leave out. So I put in everything."

Lorraine's paper was ten pages long. Her grade was a C-. Her teacher wrote, "Lorraine, you have to learn to answer the question and to leave out irrelevant information." Lorraine was confused, though. "What on earth could I have left out?"

Even social life in adolescence requires planning and organization. Skills such as making plans to go out with friends require a level of communicative and organizational skill that can confound many with AS. It's no wonder that the parents of adolescents with AS often find themselves in the role of coach, homework coordinator, social director, and hygiene monitor for their otherwise bright and accomplished offspring!

ADOLESCENCE AND EMOTIONS

Finally, adolescence presents a particular challenge because of the emotions that it provokes for individuals with AS and their families. The adolescent's growing capacity for abstract thought and self-reflection can lead to an acute awareness of being different. At an age when fitting in seems so crucial, feeling different can lead to anxiety and depression. For the less able adolescent with AS, life after high school can loom large and threatening. Even for the most able, concerns about making it, away from the protections of home and school, can feel overwhelming. The adolescents' anxieties are often no match for those of their parents, though. Parents ask, "How will she ever be able to hold a job when she can't even follow her teachers' directions?" "Will he fall in love and settle down?" "What will happen to him/her when we get sick or when we die?" Although most parents work hard to keep their anxiety to themselves, the future can seem very close and frightening to everyone involved. Managing anxiety and planning for the future become huge tasks for adolescents and families affected by AS.

SO, HOW CAN WE HELP?

When our children are young, helping is pretty easy. We can see what they need, and they readily accept our efforts to help. They usually don't mind if we do it for them. For children with neurodevelopmental disorders, our help often involves anticipating and filling their needs before they even express them. Giving the right kind of juice in the right color cup on the right place mat just makes the day flow more smoothly!

As our "children" begin the journey through adolescence, however, helping becomes more complicated. For one thing, they often have mixed feelings about our assistance. For another, they often have very definite feelings about their own opinions. As Sally once told her mother, "Just because I have Asperger's doesn't mean that you know everything I think." Most importantly, it is their life, not ours.

We can help by becoming working partners on their journeys. The ideas and strategies in this book are offered in that spirit.

A FINAL NOTE

Partners listen to each other, with their ears and their eyes. One of my partners has generously offered his experience. Please listen to his words.

Hi, my name is Ben and I am a thirteen-year-old kid in seventh grade with Aspergers Syndrome. I am going to share my experiences, and tell what it feels like to be an adolescent with Aspergers Syndrome.

There is definitely a lot of stress involved in being a kid my age with Aspergers Syndrome or even just being a kid my age. I feel tense at times and it can be hard to know when to say things.

There are a lot of things you have to know. Body language, for instance, can sometimes be the key to having friends or girl or boyfriends. Your looks—such as your hair and your clothes—are big. The way you act and feel is also big. For some kids this is hard, and for some kids this is easy. I have heard stories about a lot of kids who have almost no friends, or maybe not even any. These types of kids were not interested in kids or in people when they were younger. They had intense interests in things rather than people. Those interests can be so intense and can last for so long that by the time they reach the adolescent age they wind up without any friends.

In my situation, I am sometimes so worried about being popular and cool and having a girlfriend that my life becomes stressful. Sometimes I worry about other things that have nothing to do with being popular, like worrying if I have a disease or if the power will go out.

As a younger kid I had a lot of trouble making friends especially before my third-grade year. Before then I almost did not care. But as I got older it did matter. And I was really worried about making friends even though I had some. As I continued to get older I made some more friends and it got somewhat easier. I have been said to be luckier than most kids with the syndrome. But it's certainly not easy.

Every year after fourth grade the intensity level gets higher. You are pressured to have more friends, do more stuff with friends, be more mature, have girlfriends or boyfriends, and some of it could become a total mess for some kids. It will be hard, but if you work at it and believe in yourself, things will be okay.

What Ben didn't say, perhaps because it's second nature to him, is that the journey succeeds not just because of hard work and believing in oneself but also because he's surrounded by people who care—partners for the journey.

CHAPTER TWO

Self-Regulation and "The Four A's"

Thirteen-year-old Thomas burst out the front door as his mother and sister drove into the driveway. "I'm starving to death and I almost got killed!" he yelled. He paced around the car as his mother turned off the engine and gathered the bags from the back seat. His sister looked at him as if to say, "Not again." He continued, "I had nothing to eat. I'm starving. And I almost got killed!"

Mrs. Lee knew that there was no sense in trying to get Thomas to speak more logically until he had eaten, so she made a sandwich, poured a glass of milk, and found the chips that were hidden in the pantry. As Thomas gulped down his food (no time for Mrs. Lee to be criticizing table manners), he began to tell about his day. Pre-algebra had been rough. He had missed several problems on the quiz because he had divided wrong. "I knew how to do the stinking problems! I just divided wrong! Mrs. Smith should've known that!" Then, a cute girl was "looking at him" in computer skills class. Thomas knew that he should do something to show that he was interested, but he didn't know exactly what. By the time lunchtime came, Thomas had been on an emotional roller coaster all morning long. Then, in the lunch line, Thomas discovered that, "You forgot to give me my lunch money." He forgot the school policy that students can ask for a PB&J whenever they forget their money. He simply left the line and went to his lunch table. Unlike similar times in the past, this time Thomas didn't rant and rave. He didn't cry. He didn't draw attention to himself in any way. But he *was* hungry.

Thomas made it through the rest of the afternoon, despite his growling stomach. He said that no one noticed that he was upset and hungry. He told his mom that he was proud of his self-control, something that he had been working on because, "Cool kids don't lose their cool."

But when Thomas got to the bus, the other students were abuzz. They said that another kid had been removed from the bus and taken to the principal. Thomas didn't know who the other student was, but he was sure that he was on the same bus. He heard that the other boy had a handgun and that he had been showing bullets to other kids all day long. Thomas was certain that he was "almost killed."

Thomas was no stranger to problems on the bus. He himself had been to the principal's office for striking another student. He was relieved that someone else got in trouble too. But he was also highly anxious that he was "almost killed."

As Thomas ate and talked, his arousal level decreased slightly. It was clear to Mrs. Lee that part of the problem was that Thomas was so hungry. However, he remained "hyped up" because he was certain that he was almost killed. Mrs. Lee also knew that Thomas had about two hours of homework and a doctor's appointment. His current state wouldn't help him manage either of those tasks. Think about Thomas' day. How would you help him settle down? We'll return to see what Mrs. Lee did, after we talk about self-regulation and "The Four A's."

Thomas' behavior is a good example of the problems with self-regulation that often occur in people with Asperger Syndrome. Adolescents might not show the kicking and screaming tantrums that were frequent in childhood, but they still struggle with most aspects of self-regulation.

Self-regulation is our ability to establish and maintain the level of arousal/alertness, attention, activity, and affect (or emotion) that is appropriate for the situation at hand. It's helpful to think of self-regulation in terms of "the four A's" (arousal/alertness, attention, activity, and affect) because this can lead us to ways of helping our children.

AROUSAL/ALERTNESS

Arousal (in self-regulatory lingo) refers to how alert we are. Different levels of alertness are effective in different situations. For example, we want to be reasonably alert as we drive home late on a rainy night. But we also want to be able to settle ourselves down quickly once we get home, so that we can go to sleep easily. There seem to be certain levels of arousal that are most efficient in certain situations. Like Goldilocks' porridge, we don't want it too hot or too cold. We want it "just right." Most of us have a variety of strategies that help "perk us up" or "settle ourselves down" in efficient and socially appropriate ways.

By the way, when talking about "arousal" with adolescents, it's best to use the term "alertness"—for reasons that are probably obvious. (If you don't know the reason, ask your adolescent what arousal means to him or her!)

When we think about Thomas' day, it is clear that his arousal levels were increasing over the course of the morning. He hates making mistakes, especially in math. That began to get him "riled up." He hadn't settled down completely when the girl "looked at

Mary Sue Williams and Sherry Shellenberger talk about arousal/alertness in terms of "engine speed." When we're running too low, we're sluggish and not up to the task. We can't pay attention or concentrate. When our engine is running too high, we respond to every bit of information around us. We may still have trouble concentrating, this time because we're "hypervigilant" and distracted by every little thing. Ms. Williams and Ms. Shellenberger have written a helpful book, *How Does Your Engine Run?*, which is often used by occupational therapists. It provides lots of great ideas about understanding and changing engine speeds. The reference is available in the Resources section at the back of this book. ☀

him" in computer class. He didn't know how to interpret her behavior, but he was intrigued and excited. Intrigue, excitement, and (yes) arousal can raise the "engine speed" in most of us. By the time Thomas got to lunch, he was high as a kite. The "zigger zagger" of missing lunch money put him over the top. He literally couldn't contain his arousal level well enough to think logically and ask for a PB&J. Later in the day his "starvation" further contributed to his overload and interfered with concentration and productivity. When he heard about the boy on the bus, Thomas' arousal level went over the top. He felt as though he was almost killed, because he was already starting from a very high level of arousal.

Arousal levels are highly sensitive to the so-called "fight or flight" response. Like other mammals, human beings respond automatically to potentially dangerous situations by activating their sympathetic nervous systems. This response releases adrenaline into the body, increases heart and breathing rates, and pumps blood to our muscles to prepare us to fight off the danger or to run for our lives! Although there aren't many people-eating predators in twenty-first century America, our nervous systems still respond as though we're in as much danger as our ancestors were. For those of us lucky enough to have regulatory systems that are fairly efficient, we can consider the accuracy of our primitive fight-or-flight response before we haul off and hit the "predator" before us. For many adolescents with AS, however, the fight-or-flight response has already occurred before they have time to think about it.

Many of the fight-or-flight responses that occur for students with AS are not in reaction to life-threatening situations. In fact,

---

"Zigger zagger" is a term coined by Dr. Jane Holmes Bernstein at The Children's Hospital in Boston. It refers to any unexpected change or glitch in the day. Many families and school teams have adopted the term, as it can diffuse some of the distress over the unexpected. They teach their children and adolescents, "We'll do this and this and this, and somewhere along the way there could be a zigger zagger." Some adolescents think the term "zigger zagger" is too "babyfied." They might prefer the term "glitch." In either version, the idea is quite helpful, as it reminds all of us that there are unpredicted things in life. ✻

many of them occur in response to sensory "invasions." The feel of someone brushing against him at his locker, the smell of "hamburger surprise" in the cafeteria, the din of voices, feet, and banging locker doors during class change, the pinching elastic of her bra. Other "invasions" are social—adolescent slang, teasing, or confusion during the volleyball game in gym. Although these aren't life-threatening, the effect on the nervous system is just the same. Again and again, the "assault" of sensory intrusions and social demands can put the student in a nearly constant state of fight-or-flight. When the student's arousal level is at a high pitch already, it doesn't take much to put him or her "over the edge." Even well-intentioned and good-natured joking around can be the last straw. Unfortunately, the resulting behavior often looks like an overreaction to the outside observer.

Although it's challenging to deal with the fight-or-flight reaction that looks like an emotional outburst, the reaction of "shutdown" is even more perplexing. Sometimes students may look lethargic and "out of it" and we're tempted to do things to perk them up. We provide all kinds of stimulation in an effort to wake up the child's nervous system. But for some youngsters, withdrawal and that dazed look really mean that the child has gone over the top. In other words, he or she has become so overwhelmed by input that shutdown and withdrawal are the only options. In this case, the adolescent needs calming, not alerting, input.

SO, HOW CAN WE HELP?

Think of a suspension bridge across the river. It's a beautifully designed structure that gleams in the morning sun. When it stands alone, with no load on it, it is strong and effective. As the cars begin to cross over, the bridge feels the added load. It may begin to groan and sway a little, but it still stands. Later in the day, though, the truckers start to cross. The bridge sways and groans more. It was designed to hold load, though, and it manages. But then rush hour comes, the cars pile up, the eighteen-wheelers idle. The bridge is really stressed. It may still manage to hold, however, as long as the weather is calm. As rush hour proceeds, a wind comes up. The bluster of the wind, the load of the cars and trucks, and the lack of time for recovery are too much. The cables snap and vehicles begin to tumble. This is the brain of the adolescent with AS. It works beautifully in so many situations. But when the mental equivalent of the eighteen-wheelers and blustery wind strikes, overload occurs.

In partnership with our adolescents, we can help with the overload by using a five-part approach.

1. **Identify the signs of overload in the adolescent.** Some individuals go from "zero to sixty" in a few seconds. Others build up gradually. Careful observation and comparing notes with others can help us understand the adolescent's unique responses to growing load. One teenager I know begins to rock slightly in his chair when his arousal level starts to rise. If he's unable to settle himself, the next observable reaction is slight hand-flapping (usually below the table or desk, because he's learned that flapping isn't cool). His voice volume starts to rise, and the tone becomes more insistent. If his overload continues, he begins to pace back and forth across the room, talking to himself under his breath. On rare occasions, when no one recognizes his distress, he may hit out at others. This hitting only occurs as a last resort, however, when neither he nor anyone around him can reorganize his arousal and affect.

2. **Identify the situations that are most likely to be problematic.** Consider the environmental characteristics of the situation that puts the adolescent at risk for overload (for example, noise level, smells, crowds). Consider the demands upon the adolescent (such as social demands or cognitive/thinking demands). Think about the behavior of other people in the situation (for example, loud or fast-paced talking, harsh tones of voice). Don't forget to consider *when* the situation occurs. Remember that "load" is cumulative—in other words, it builds up over the course of the day or week (or sometimes, month).

3. **Identify the strategies that the adolescent is already using to manage his or her arousal level.** How efficient are these? Do they actually lead to a level of arousal that works in the situation? How appropriate are the strategies to the social demands of the situation? (For example, chewing on rubber

tubing may be a great strategy for a seven-year-old, but it looks "weird" when used by a middle schooler.)

4. **Determine ways that the environment could be modified to reduce the load.** This has to be done in partnership with the adolescent. Some of our "greatest ideas" might embarrass them to death. Some modifications are easy, such as changing his locker to the end of the row (where he doesn't get jostled as much) or letting her sit at the back of computer class (where others don't notice how slowly she types). Other modifications may be more difficult to sell. For example, I've worked for years to convince high school teachers that it is okay to provide class notes for the student with AS. Once the teachers are convinced, they find that the student pays better attention to their lectures because he or she is not as overwhelmed by the task of listening, deciding what is important, writing it down, and then tuning back in to the lecture. (More about note taking in Chapters Four and Five.)

   Perhaps the most important environmental modifications are related to the behavior of the adults in the situation. When we come across as critical or impatient, we actually risk retriggering the fight-or-flight response in the adolescent. Thus, it is crucial for us to understand **"LOW and SLOW."** In fact, for adolescents with AS, LOW and SLOW may be the most helpful modification of all. LOW and SLOW is described on page 30.

5. **Finally, teach the adolescent how to read his or her own sensations and behavior and how to manage arousal levels most effectively and appropriately.** As described by other authors, this teaching is most helpful when it provides "rules" that the adolescent can apply to certain situations. For example, a student may learn that when she feels her shoulders creeping up around her ears, that's a good signal that she's getting overloaded. When she feels that signal, her best bet is to take five slow deep breaths and push her shoulders down and back in "ballet dancer posture." She can then focus on deep breathing and ballet dancer posture until she feels her body relax. Other students respond to teaching such as, "Math class is often tough. Before I go in, I need to eat ten Skittles and get a drink

of water." Some adolescents will practice progressive muscle relaxation, imagery, or meditation. Obviously, such strategies won't be successful unless the student's educational team is on board. The team must convince the student through words and behavior that it really is all right to use these techniques. In fact, the most convincing arguments often come from the teachers who model self-regulatory strategies and encourage the whole class to use them!

ATTENTION

Many adolescents with AS have been diagnosed with attention-deficit hyperactivity aisorder (ADHD) at some time in their lives. But most of their parents feel that ADHD alone just doesn't fit their child. This is often because the child can pay rapt attention to so many topics and activities.

We're learning that the attention problems of most individuals with AS are slightly different from those of children with "garden variety ADHD." Students with AS can pay attention pretty well. They just can't regulate or shift their attention efficiently. He may still be focused on whether the trains that took U.S. troops across the country were steam or diesel when the teacher has moved on to the importance of troop deployment and supply lines in the Civil War. She may have trouble listening to her mother's directions regarding what needs to be done in "that room of yours" because she is still figuring out how her favorite rock star managed to dye her hair such a great shade of pastel pink. Certainly most adolescents have to be brought back from "space" intermittently. Adolescents with AS just need to be brought back more frequently than most.

Adolescents with AS also have trouble regulating their attention when they're in a state of fight-or-flight. As we discussed above, it's hard to pay attention when your engine is racing—there are too many thoughts, too many feelings, and too many sensations. For adolescents with AS, the sensory load can become overwhelming. When it comes right down to it, how can you pay attention to your teacher or parent when your jeans are digging into your waist? Or,

LOW and SLOW

"LOW and SLOW" refers to the way in which we should approach children and adolescents who are in distress (or becoming so). It is based on our understanding of the fight-or-flight response and what serves to calm people and other mammals. It is also based upon the recognition that most of us become distressed when our children are distressed or disorganized. In these situations, most of us find that our own engines rev. While this is understandable, it doesn't help our kids. In fact, agitated or intense behavior on the part of the adults usually intensifies the distress and disorganization of our kids. LOW and SLOW is a strategy for helping us modify our own behavior in order to give our children and ourselves a chance of settling down.

LOW. . .

○ Lower your body so that your eyes are at or below the eye level of the child. If the adolescent might hit or kick you in the course of his distress, make sure that you stay at a safe distance.

○ Lower your voice—both in volume and in pitch. Keep your tone matter of fact, even if you're screaming on the inside.

○ Lower the complexity of your language. Speak in short sentences. Don't ask a lot of questions. Don't preach.

SLOW . . .

○ Slow down your own heart rate and breathing rate. This is usually accomplished most easily by taking slow, deep breaths (count to yourself "In-2-3-4, Out-2-3-4-5-6").

○ Slow down your rate of speech. Pause between sentences. In these situations, I try to speak no more than once every 30 to 60 seconds.

○ Slow down your movements. We mammals feel threatened by sudden movement. If you must move quickly (such as when a child is in danger), try to do so in full view of the child.

○ Slow down your agenda. Take your time. It takes as long as it takes. If you (or the child) need to be somewhere soon, let someone else know that you may be late. If you can't do that, announce calmly to the child that you will have to make a change at a certain time. Make a transition plan such as, "We can sit quietly until the next bell rings to tell us that your classmates are coming in. Then we'll take ten deep breaths together and move to a more private spot."

THE NEXT STEP . . .

○ Once the adolescent begins to settle down, you can make objective and descriptive comments such as, "Boy, were you angry. Your face was redder than I've ever seen it."

○ Try to refrain from asking questions at this point. The load of answering "why" questions can retrigger fight-or-flight.

○ If you have an idea about what happened, make a guess. "I'm not sure, because I'm not in your body. (Pause.) But it looked like you got really agitated because the mall was so noisy and crowded." Always propose your idea in the spirit of a hypothesis.

○ If the adolescent starts to talk about his/her reactions, listen. Don't try to fix things or offer solutions.

○ Do the problem solving and talk about consequences (if any) at a later time, after everyone is calm.

DON'T . . .

○ Try to process the situation or teach a lesson when the adolescent is still agitated or distressed.

○ Announce negative consequences at this point.

○ Make threats such as "If you don't settle down right now, I'll . . . . "

○ Think you're letting the adolescent "escape" anything. None of us thinks and remembers clearly when we're in a state of agitation. Talking about morals, values, and consequences at this point just ends up frustrating the adult.

○ Worry about what other people will think.

○ Think that this will go on forever. This is one strategy in which "an ounce of prevention is worth a pound of cure." Through the adult's use of LOW and SLOW, adolescents learn that there are people who can bear witness to their agitation and be helpful. It makes it easier for them to seek help in the future.

to recall an old Hanes underwear commercial, "You can't think right when your underwear's too tight." If we use the word "underwear" as a symbol for any discomfort, it's amazing that some of our kids can ever pay attention to what we think is important.

Finally, many adolescents with AS have trouble regulating their attention because they haven't identified what to listen for or what to look at. In a sea of words, they seize upon those that sound familiar and promising but they tend to miss the "gist." They really are paying attention. It's just not to the stuff we consider important.

SO, HOW CAN WE HELP?

Strategies that assist adolescents in regulating their attention are based upon the assumption that we've also used the five-part approach described above. Of course the specific modifications and interventions will differ from one adolescent to another, but these are some ideas that have worked for others.

MODIFICATIONS OF THE ENVIRONMENT AND COMMUNICATION STYLE

○ Remember that many individuals with AS cannot make eye contact and listen at the same time. Don't assume that she isn't listening to you when her head is on her desk. She may simply need to shut down the visual channel in order to attend to your voice.

○ Reduce unnecessary distractions. In the classroom, put old tennis balls on the feet of the chairs to reduce noise. Consider using full spectrum lights to eliminate the flicker of fluorescent lights. Have the student sit in the spot where he or she feels least distracted (this may not be the same spot we would choose). At home, allow the adolescent to create a homework space that is most "comfy." If listening to music helps block out other household noises, then allow the stereo or boom box (radio stations are usually too distracting).

○ Whenever possible, give instructions first in the sensory channel that is most efficient for the adolescent. For most students with AS, this is the auditory/language channel. They benefit from a verbal explanation prior to having to analyze a visual array such as a chart or graph. Be careful, though, about assuming that the auditory/language channel is most efficient—some youngsters with AS fool us.

○ Provide auditory frames for the adolescent's attention. Follow the Dale Carnegie rule of public speaking: "Tell them what you're going to say. Then say it. Then tell them what you said." Announce the topic of the discussion before beginning to speak. Tell the student what to listen for. In the classroom, it may help to provide a graphic organizer (or chart) with a very simple outline of the "listening points." If you're going to make more than one point, hold up the relevant number of fingers (for example, "There are three parts to this argument"). Then, as you're speaking, hold up the number of fingers that corresponds to the item number you're discussing. (By the way, that also helps us remember what we're doing!) At home and at school, don't overload the adolescent's attention and memory with directions. Allow the adolescent to finish following the first set of directions before giving the next.

○ Provide visual frames for attention. In the classroom, use an overhead projector and screen to highlight the place where the student is supposed to look. If that isn't workable, outline the space on your blackboard or whiteboard where new material will always be presented. This makes it easier for the student to return to the visual demonstration efficiently when his or her attention wanders. At home, help the student begin with a clear workspace. When talking about feelings or problems, do so in an environment that reduces visual stimulation (in other words, don't do it when the TV is on).

○ Use graphic organizers and task cards to help the adolescent stay focused on the *relevant* aspects of the task at hand. Reinforce him or her for completion of steps or "chunks" of the task, not just for completion of the entire activity. (Examples of graphic organizers and task cards for adolescents can be found in Chapter Five.)

○ Model goal-directed activity. If you've told him to do his homework, don't interrupt with questions about whether he needs gym clothes for tomorrow. If you've decided that you're going to pay the bills, comment to her that you're tempted to stop for a cup of coffee but that you're trying to stay on track.

STRATEGIES THAT PROMOTE MORE EFFICIENT
REGULATION OF ATTENTION

○ Teach the adolescent to make sure his "engine speed" is appropriate for the task at hand. For example, if she's feeling sluggish, she might need to have a crunchy snack or dance to a favorite song before sitting down to work.

○ Teach the adolescent to inhibit irrelevant thoughts, feelings, or reactions. This is an important part of paying attention—if we can't inhibit (or stop) our reactions to irrelevant or unimportant information, we can't pay attention to the situation at hand. This problem of inhibition can be quite apparent in conversations with adolescents with AS; they don't inhibit their thoughts, and then they take us on a wild goose chase of a discussion. One way to teach inhibition is to give direct feedback to the adolescent: "Wait a minute! I thought we were talking about weekend plans. Now you're talking about the *Titanic*. Let's finish talking about weekend plans, then you can tell me about the *Titanic*." I've found many adolescents begin to echo my words, "It's not time to talk about ____, we're talking about ____."

○ "OHIO"—"Only Handle It Once." If possible, finish one thing before moving on to the next. If the adolescent begins math homework, this isn't a good time to look for the catalog that tells the model number of the Santa Fe railroad engine that he wants for Christmas.

○ Break the task into chunks. Adolescents of all stripes (especially the younger ones) need help with this. We can help them break down the task into chunks and then teach them to reinforce themselves for completing each chunk. For example, "First I'll do problems 1–10, then I'll check on that model number." Checking on the model number becomes a "natural reinforcement" for completing a chunk of work.

○ For many adolescents, especially those of superior intellectual ability, school tasks can take forever because they don't know what to leave out. Help them learn to use outlines or other graphic organizers to ensure that they have attended to the critical parts of the assignment.

○ Help the adolescent identify the crucial aspects of social interaction. For example, if a friend is coming over, remind the adolescent that it's important to listen to what the friend has to say and what the friend wants to do. Caution the adolescent that he shouldn't ignore the friend in order to focus on the CNN stock market reports.

○ Finally (and perhaps most importantly) teach the adolescent socially appropriate strategies that he or she can use when it is simply impossible to deploy attention efficiently. Lines such as "Excuse me, Mrs. Jones. I'm having a terrible time concentrating. Can I go get a drink of water?" or "Dad, I can't focus on you right now. I'm stuck on the stock market. Can I just tell you about the NASDAQ, then we'll talk about my driving test?"

ACTIVITY

As we've already discussed, many adolescents with AS have a history of an ADHD diagnosis. This isn't simply because of their attentional problems, but also because many of them had trouble regulating their activity levels. Again, though, this wasn't garden variety ADHD. Instead, many adolescents with AS go from being "hyper" or agitated to being sluggish. Some adolescents with AS never reach the "hyper" level, but instead remain perpetually lethargic. Add to this the adolescent fatigue associated with rapid physical growth and we can have quite a challenge!

As with attention, the problem of activity level for adolescents with AS is not so much one of over- or underactivity. Instead, it's a matter of being at the right activity level for the situation. When Thomas comes to my office and paces back and forth, squats on the loveseat, or tosses Koosh balls in the air, it's hard for

him to do problem solving. But, when told that he has to sit
down so that I don't lose my mind, he flops onto the loveseat
cushions and "zones out." It's not a matter of Thomas' being
rude. It's a matter of his not being able to get to "just right" in his
activity level.

SO, HOW CAN WE HELP?

All of the modifications and interventions discussed for managing arousal are crucial to the regulation of activity. Other helpful
techniques include:

○ Remember that physical activity is seldom quelled by a "top
  down" approach such as "Calm down." Instead, "bottom
  up" approaches such as slow, rhythmic activities, deep
  breathing, instrumental music (not rap!), and walking are
  more effective. Brainstorm with the adolescent about what
  works best for him or her.
○ Tolerate reasonable amounts of movement. Don't expect
  the adolescent to sit still (or to sit up straight). If he can't sit
  in a chair without leaning back on two legs, put elastic
  bands around the rungs of the chair and have him push his
  feet against those.
○ Provide motor breaks frequently. Whenever possible, have
  the adolescent do "heavy work" during the break. Have
  your son or daughter carry the laundry basket up or down
  the stairs. At school, send her on an errand to the office or
  library. One art teacher I know sends a student to the store-
  room for 20 pounds of clay on a regular basis.
○ Ensure that the adolescent engages in some form of physical activity on a regular basis. Since many students with AS
  are clumsy and averse to team sports, you may have to be
  creative in the physical activity department. However, many
  adolescents with AS do enjoy non-team sports such as
  swimming, skiing, hiking, bowling, horseback riding, and
  karate or t'ai chi.
○ In the classroom, engage everyone in chair or wall push-
  ups, stretching, and deep breathing.

○ Teach the adolescent to understand what his or her body needs in order to be reasonably well controlled. Talk about what he/she uses to meet those needs. (One 12-year-old told me that he had to move to think!) Then brainstorm about developmentally appropriate (or "cool") ways to accomplish the same purpose.

AFFECT

"Affect" refers to the emotional tone or feeling that's attached to a thought or event. When we talk about the regulation of affect, we're really talking about the ability to manage our emotions in a socially and developmentally appropriate way. Given that the feelings associated with fight-or-flight are anger and fear, it's not surprising that adolescents who have trouble regulating arousal often have difficulty controlling the accompanying feelings.

Think back to Thomas' difficult day. Thomas was having trouble regulating his arousal and activity throughout the day, for a whole host of reasons. By the time he got to the bus, he was a bundle of nerves and probably ready to let down his defenses. But the story about the boy with the gun sent his arousal level skyrocketing. His initial reaction was one of panic, and he had trouble letting go of that reaction for hours to come. Despite the logical discrepancies between what actually happened and Thomas' reaction, it's important to note that he really couldn't let go of the incident or of his fear. Add that to the overload associated with his "starvation" and it's apparent why homework time was a bust that night.

SO, HOW CAN WE HELP?

Working with adolescents to manage affect rests upon setting into motion many of the strategies listed above. In particular, it's critical to follow the five-part approach to overarousal and to remember LOW and SLOW. However, it's also important to help the adolescent learn to interpret social situations and his/her own reactions in a more accurate manner. (The specifics of this will be discussed in Chapters Three, Six, Seven, and Eight.)

In the meantime, let's talk about what happened to Thomas.

For better or worse, Thomas had a psychotherapy appointment that day. He began the session by announcing that he had missed lunch and that he was "almost killed." Understanding Thomas' need for basic comforts such as food, I first offered food. Thomas and his mother reassured me that he had eaten enough that he was no longer starving. Although he was no longer hungry and had taken a forty-five minute drive to the office, Thomas was still aroused. He paced back and forth. His voice was at near maximum volume. He found a soft block that had a bell inside and tossed that from hand to hand and back and forth across the room. Although he wanted to talk about how he was "almost killed," he couldn't settle down enough to talk. I considered setting limits (especially since the bell and the foam block were distracting me), but I remembered LOW and SLOW. As I commented upon his behavior and his obvious mixed feelings about talking about the incident, Thomas settled down very gradually. Finally, he was able to tell his story about being "almost killed." As he spoke, it was clear that Thomas really believed that he had been in danger, although he hadn't seen the student in question, nor did he think he even knew him. He wasn't able to see that he really had been nowhere near danger, if any had really existed in the first place. Thomas also was unable to understand that the other kids on the bus might have been making up stories, especially as bomb threats had been rather frequent in the neighboring town. Thomas was unswayed in his belief that he had almost been killed.

Adhering to the theory "if you can't beat them, join them," I switched to a discussion of what Thomas could do if another student brought a gun to school. How could he stay calm? Whom should he tell? Where should he go? Thomas also needed to talk about why a student would want to bring a gun to school. Did it mean that the other kid was very angry? Who was he mad at? What if Thomas got that angry? Would somebody stop him?

Thomas left the session in slightly better shape. It took him about a week to recover entirely. He needed to talk with his parents more that night. He needed to talk about it with his best friend. He needed the reassurance of seeing what the school administration would do. He still wasn't sure that the school had told them "the whole truth," but he was reassured enough to let the topic drop. Most importantly, Thomas felt reassured that he would know what to do if something like that happened again. He also knew what to do if he felt that angry.

A FINAL NOTE

Self-regulation is a lifelong journey for all of us. We're better at it during some phases of our lives and worse during other times. All kinds of life stressors can throw our tried and true strategies into disarray. During adolescence, change occurs at an increasingly rapid pace and many of the strategies that worked for us as children are no longer acceptable, much less cool. In this regard, adolescents with AS are quite similar to their non-AS classmates. In fact, walking through the halls of a middle or high school during class change can make one wonder whether an entire generation of children has lost the capacity to self-regulate! Of course, our parents probably thought we were even worse when we screamed and cried for John, Paul, George, and Ringo or their latter-day equivalents.

Our task, as the grownups, is to be working partners with all of our children as they find regulatory strategies that are comfortable, flexible, and at least reasonably appropriate. For our adolescents with AS, we must simply remember that their journey may be more challenging and that they may need more support and guidance along the way. For ourselves, we must remember that they're not doing it *to* us. Like all of us, they're simply doing the best they can with the nervous systems they have.

CHAPTER THREE

"You Can't Not Communicate"

Overheard in the high school hallway:
Christina: "So, he said, well, y'know, 'Way.' And I said, 'No way.'"
Jenna: "You did? You go, girl."
Christina: "Well, I just couldn't deal."
Jenna: "He's a poser, anyway."

The title of this chapter, "You Can't Not Communicate," comes from the first textbook I read on doing psychotherapy. The author (whose name I can't recall) used the forbidden double negative ("can't not") to emphasize that we're all communicating all the time. In fact, our communication is multisensory—including the auditory aspects of words and sentences, the auditory components of tone of voice and other sounds (sighs, pauses, and so on), the visual aspects of facial expression and body language, and sometimes the aspects of touch (as when someone touches our arm or hugs us).

All of this information allows us to try to answer the question, "What was Christina and Jenna's conversation about?" As parents and teachers of adolescents, we can make a lot of guesses. Some of our guesses make us want to echo, "You go, girl." Whatever "Way" was, we're glad Christina said, "No way." Our guesses may or may not be correct, but we do have enough communicative skill to fill in the blanks in the conversation between Christina and Jenna.

Christina and Jenna don't have AS. What happens to the high school girl in the midst of this communicative environment if she does have AS?

Most adolescents with AS have excellent vocabularies. Their grammar is usually good. In fact, their spontaneous communication may be much less vague than that of Christina and Jenna! Adolescents with AS usually struggle with what we call the **pragmatics** of communication—how we use words, grammar, and nonverbal expression to convey our thoughts, wishes, and feelings. It's the pragmatic challenge that makes it hard for the adolescent with AS to understand Christina and Jenna. So, where do these pragmatics break down for adolescents with AS?

INTENTIONS AND MEANING

Adolescents with AS understand and express ideas most efficiently when everything is concrete and definite. They would work well with Sergeant Bill Friday on that old TV show *Dragnet*: "Just the facts, ma'am, just the facts."

But, look back to Christina and Jenna. Is there a fact in the conversation? Is there a concrete word in the whole conversation? Unless you count "poser" (which we'll come back to), Christina and Jenna rely entirely on vague words to convey what seems like some very dramatic intention and meaning.

Adolescents without AS know what Christina and Jenna were talking about from the context of the conversation, from Christina's tone of voice and body language, and from their own social awareness. Adolescents with AS may not have noticed the context cues (Christina had been going out with Joe, a fact known to "everybody") or the nonverbal cues (Christina's eyes are red, her voice is shaky). They may not have noticed the growing sense of sexual urgency among the senior class. Even if adolescents with AS had noticed some of these bits of information, it would be difficult for them to put it all together and to sense the confusing feelings that Christina expresses. One of my adolescent girls stated, "If a guy asks me to do something wrong, I just say, 'Go jump off a bridge.' If it's wrong, it's wrong. Period. End of discussion." While this response is a parent's dream in many ways, it doesn't equip the adolescent for the "gray areas" of adolescent and adult life.

For an adolescent with AS, understanding the messages of others is also challenging because of slang and abstract language. Think again about Christina and Jenna. What does "way" mean? What's a "poser"? And why is Jenna telling Christina to "go"? All of these words are used in an abstract manner. Even though we are encrusted with age (according to our adolescent offspring), we're able to figure out the intended meaning. But adolescents with AS often aren't able to "bend their minds" around multiple meanings and abstractions.

Think of this scenario between twelve-year-old Mark Larkin and his mother.

Mark, his mother, and his two younger brothers were driving to the local ice-cream stand. As they approached, Mark noticed that the marquee proclaimed, "We have BAD ice cream!"

Mrs. Larkin thought, "Oh no. Here we go."

As if on cue, Mark said, "Mom, look! They say the ice cream is bad. We'd better go somewhere else."

Mrs. Larkin proceeded to try to explain the slang meaning of "bad." Even Mark's nine-year-old brother added his own wisdom about slang. They talked about how "wicked" doesn't always mean "evil." They talked about how everyone knows that this ice-cream stand has terrific ice cream. After about ten minutes of talking, Mark agreed that they could get ice-cream cones.

Mark loves ice cream and can't talk while he's eating his beloved pistachio. After he finished his cone, he said, "Mom, I finally get it." Mrs. Larkin breathed a sigh of relief and asked what he thought.

"You know how you always tell us that too much ice cream is bad for our teeth and health? And you know how this place is always so crowded?" he began. "Well, I think the owner decided that he would help kids out by telling them that the ice cream is bad. Then they won't be bugging their parents to get it so often. And he also thought that this would be a way to get rid of some of the crowds. Did you notice that this place isn't as crowded as usual? I guess his plan worked."

Mrs. Larkin sighed. "I'll have to keep working on this one," she thought.

By the way, a few months into seventh grade, Mark decided to write a "Dictionary of Double Meanings." He fascinated his peers, teachers, and parents with off-the-beaten-path expressions and slang. In making the topic a passion, he gained mastery, competence, and the esteem of others!

Adolescents with AS have challenges in understanding communicative intent in written language as well. This difficulty in reading comprehension may not have appeared in elementary school, because the reading selections were more concrete and the questions more factual.

Consider this assignment: Seventh graders were asked to answer comprehension questions on a set of five chapters from Clemence McLaren's *Inside the Walls of Troy*, a novel read in Social Studies. One of the questions was "Why did Helen's father lose all interest in ruling Sparta?" The answer could be found in the following paragraph:

"When Menelaus returned to claim me, he found himself doubly blessed. Not only was he marrying the world's most beautiful woman, he was inheriting a kingdom as well. My father had lost all interest in kingship after the death of his sons. He wanted to retire to his hunting lodge. After our marriage Menelaus and I would rule Sparta in his stead." (p. 42 1998, Clemence McLaren)

A student with concrete communication skills would probably answer: "Helen's father had lost all interest in kingship after the death of his sons" (copying the answer directly from the text). A student who truly understood communication (and human feelings) would write, "Helen's father was too sad to rule. He just wanted to get away." While the first answer is sufficient, it doesn't really show that the student understood what was going on with the people in the book. This challenge in understanding people is a hallmark of AS, and it becomes more striking during the adolescent years.

The good news is that adolescents with AS often become intrigued with figures of speech, multiple meanings, and slang once we give them a translation guide. Many of the adolescents I know are fabulous punsters. Their wry sense of humor is delightful—illustrating the strength of their thinking and the energy they devote to anything that fascinates them.

UNDERSTANDING THE MENTAL STATE OF OTHERS

As demonstrated in the conversation between Christina and Jenna, typically developing adolescents are skilled in making inferences about the mental state of the people around them. This is partly a matter of empathy, being able to feel with the other person even if you haven't had the same experience yourself. (We'll talk more about empathy in Chapters Eight and Nine.) It's also a matter of knowing what the other person might or might not know about what you're saying.

These aspects of communication have been studied in the context of **Theory of Mind** (ToM), a person's ability to make inferences about the mental state of someone else. The research is inconsistent, sometimes showing that adolescents with Asperger's do fine on ToM tests and sometimes showing real challenges. Talk to a parent or typically developing sibling of an adolescent with AS, though, and there's no doubt: the adolescent with AS "doesn't get it."

Eighteen-year-old Tim walked into the office without the usual social niceties. There was no "Hello" or "How are you today?" His first words were: "I just can't get that incident out of my mind. I thought he was a good guy and then he did that. Ever since then, I haven't been able to trust people."

I was confused. What incident? Who was "he"? What did "he" do?

"Wait a minute, Tim. You've lost me. I can't figure out what you're talking about."

"You can't?" said Tim. "Well, I was thinking about this all the way to your office."

This vignette demonstrates a common problem for individuals with AS. They often are unable to make accurate assumptions about what another person knows. Since Tim had been thinking about the incident all the way to the office, he assumed that I knew what he was thinking. He wasn't able to step back and realize that he hadn't shared any of these thoughts and feelings with me and that I had no way of guessing. I was able to get up to speed by asking Tim questions about the incident and who was involved. We were then able to talk about Tim's confusion and hurt. We were even able to talk about other similar experiences. But arriving at a mutual understanding of what was happening depended upon my ability to structure the communication, not upon Tim's.

Parents of children and adolescents with AS frequently report that their offspring make inaccurate assumptions about what others know or don't know. Some of these communication errors are in the direction of assuming that listeners know more than they actually do (as in the case of Tim). At other times, the communicative slip-up occurs because the adolescent assumes that the listener knows nothing or forgets that he has told the story before (sometimes countless times). While our usual social customs would suggest that we should listen politely, no matter what the social error, most parents finally realize that they must provide corrective feedback or their child will make similar errors in "the real world."

CONVERSATIONAL SKILLS

Even before they can talk, typically developing babies seem to understand that human interaction involves give and take, "conversational turn taking." They wait, in anticipation of our reaction. They respond, in a way that is connected somehow to what we do.

By school age, most children are able to incorporate verbal and nonverbal information into a rich, fast-paced conversational style. Although they go off-track fairly often, they do seem to understand the idea that other people get a turn to talk every once in a while!

Children and adolescents with Asperger Syndrome may have an unusual conversational style—often like feast or famine. Their ideas flow as long as they have "topic control." They are able to regale others with their knowledge of their current passions. They often present information that others hadn't even thought about. Yet, the same person can be tongue-tied when asked to respond to "simple" questions such as "What did you do in school today?" Now, all of us know that most kids answer the school question with "I dunno" or "Nothing."

But the typically developing adolescent can formulate answers when he understands that the other person is really interested in the answer. The typically developing adolescent is also skilled in reciprocation, asking the conversational partner about his or her experiences and feelings. Adolescents with AS struggle with staying on a topic that someone else starts, because this requires them to regulate their attention and behavior (see Chapter Two). They also have trouble staying on topic because of their difficulties in understanding the other person's state of mind. They have trouble reading the rhythm of the conversation, and they don't know when it's okay to introduce a new topic.

By the way, when we're talking about adolescent communication, we have to distinguish between "can't" and "don't want to." Typically developing adolescents can engage in long, connected conversations (witness their phone calls or "instant messages"); they just may not want to do so with their parents or teachers. Adolescents with AS often cannot engage in "connected discourse," even when they do want to.

Adolescents with AS are often accused of interrupting. They don't see it as interrupting, though. They've learned in speech therapy that they have to wait for a pause in the other person's language. When they hear silence, they assume that they can speak. They aren't able to infer whether the other person has completed his or her thought. This is particularly apparent during a three- (or more)-way conversation. The rhythm and complexity of multiple speakers and multiple listeners overwhelm their sensory and communicative capacities and lead to a number of conversational faux pas.

COMMUNICATIVE CONVENTIONS (ALSO KNOWN AS "MANNERS")

If manners were innate, Miss Manners and Amy Vanderbilt would be out of business. As all of us know, respecting and using polite communication is a lifelong task. Even the most "typical" among us break the social rules more often than we admit to our children.

That said, it is also apparent that adolescents with AS break the rules even more often than do their agemates. It's not that they were raised in a barn. It's not that they want to offend others. It's not that they are disrespectful of people in authority. Their communicative rulebreaking seems to arise from several sources: their self-regulatory glitches, which often keep them from being able to think before they speak; their difficulties in reading the situation; their inefficiencies in controlling voice volume and tone; their awkward body language; and their limited understanding of the effect of their actions upon others.

Never forget: It's not about disrespect, it's about inefficiency!

Fourteen-year-old Matt and other students were working on a social studies worksheet at their desks. The teacher was talking with a small group of students who were planning their project on ancient Asian civilizations. The teaching assistant was sitting at a table at the side of the room, calling out questions to a student who had missed the pop quiz in class yesterday.

Matt came upon a question he didn't understand. He called out to the assistant, "I need you." The assistant, Mrs. McGonigle, held up one finger as though to say, "Just a minute." Matt fumed. He tore a sheet out of his notebook and wrote Mrs. McGonigle a note: "You are MY assistant. You're supposed to be here for ME. Meet me and Dr. Bolick at 11."

When I arrived at 11, Matt was still angry. Mrs. McGonigle was appalled at Matt's "disrespectful" behavior. Even if she had done something wrong (and she didn't know what that might have been), Matt had no right to write such a disrespectful note.

As the story of the incident was told, it became clear that Matt didn't know what Mrs. McGonigle meant when she held up one finger. Even when we explained it to him, he couldn't understand why Mrs. McGonigle couldn't come immediately to him. Explanations such as "Mrs. McGonigle will come to you when she reaches a good stopping point" were useless, as Matt didn't know what a "good stopping point" would be. We had to go through countless examples of how Matt could tell when Mrs. McGonigle would help him ("If I get to your desk at the same time as Eric, who will you help first?" "If Eric gets there a microsecond before me, will you help him first?"). Matt wasn't just being a pain—he truly didn't get it. We couldn't move from the specific to a general rule ("Mrs. McGonigle will come to you as soon as she can.") until we had practiced many specific combinations.

When we finally established how Matt would know when Mrs. McGonigle could help him and what he could do in the meantime (for example, go on to the next question), we had to tackle the more difficult aspect of the situation. How could we help Matt understand that he needed to use different communicative styles for different people? How could we help him understand that no matter how wrong he thought an adult's behavior was, he needed to be polite? How could we help him understand that tone of voice and body language are an important part of communicating with people in different stations life? (We'll talk in a later chapter about how to teach adolescents what to do when the adult's behavior is *really* wrong.)

SO, HOW CAN WE HELP?

Remember what Liane Willey wrote, "Small group conversations make my nerves feel like they are wearing stilts on icy pavement" (p. 37). We can help adolescents with AS by doing the communicative equivalent of drying up the icy pavement *and* teaching them to walk on stilts. This involves several tasks. First we must ensure that they are regulated enough to be available for communication. This involves the modifications and interventions discussed in Chapter Two. Secondly, we must ensure that they are willing to be partners with us on this "mini-journey." Third, we must modify our own styles to give them a chance of understanding what we're trying to communicate. We want our adolescents to learn to manage all types of communication eventually, but we have to continue to provide scaffolding until they begin to master these skills. Finally, we must be prepared to act as an interpreter of those nuances of "neurotypical" communication and as an instructor in the communication "Rules of the Road."

MODIFICATIONS OF (OUR OWN) COMMUNICATIVE STYLE

○ The most important element of communication with adolescents with AS is the creation of a warm and trusting relationship. We must let them know that we're fallible, too, and that we're not in it to preach. For example, when sixteen-year-old Mary came in last week, she was in a foul mood. Everything I said was met with a scowl. Though my "adult vibes" were screaming "Disrespect!" I know that Mary isn't so grouchy unless something has gone wrong. I attempted to make a bridge between us, telling her about the Beatles special and how the commentator had talked with some of the members of the band 'N Sync. I thought this would pull Mary in, as I remembered that she's a big 'N Sync fan. When Mary gave me one of those "You're clueless" looks, it clicked. Her favorite band is No Doubt, not 'N Sync. I exclaimed, "Oh Mary! I had another senior moment! I was thinking 'N Sync is your band, but it's No Doubt, isn't it?" Mary laughed heartily. She thought it was great that she isn't the only one with communication and memory problems.

She was then able to talk about how she didn't understand what her classmates meant when they said they wanted to be friends but then never returned her phone calls.

We must never forget that the most effective communication occurs in the context of a relationship.

○ Whenever possible, be congruent. This means that your words and nonverbal signals match your intended message. Don't be "sicky sweet" to adolescents. It never convinces them, even those with AS. Remember, though, that your intensity can overload adolescents with AS. We have to exert significant self-control in order to let them know what we mean without overwhelming them with affect (see LOW and SLOW in Chapter Two).

○ If you're annoyed or frustrated, try to "metacommunicate" about your feelings. "You know, when you did that, I felt really mad. But I know that you can't understand me very well when I'm ranting and raving. Can we talk about what happened?" Remember that debriefing about what happened usually can't occur until the adolescent (and the adult) settle down.

○ Try not to say too much too fast. Pause between critical ideas or instructions. Allow the adolescent to process the first thing you say before you move on to the next thing.

○ When asking a question, provide plenty of processing time before repeating or rephrasing. (I often count to fifteen in my head.)

○ Be prepared to provide extra "scaffolding" in group conversations. Limit the number of abstract terms that the student has to process. For example, tell the class to answer each question in two complete sentences, rather than "go the extra mile." Avoid sarcasm whenever possible.

○ Be direct about what you want the adolescent to do. Most adolescents with AS don't change their behavior in response to indirect communication such as "My goodness, Sarah, you certainly seem to have a lot to say about this." Instead, Sarah needs to be told, "Sarah, you've answered a lot of questions. It's time to give someone else a chance."

○ Be clear. In fact, be clearer than clear. When Tim was 20, he had a job in a bookstore. When there were no customers at the cash register, Tim sat on a stool and "relaxed." His manager was dismayed and told Tim that he needed to "look around and see what needed to be done." When Tim continued to sit on the stool, the manager gently confronted him. Tim's reply was that he did look around, but that he didn't see anything that needed to be done. The manager then made a list of things to do when no one was in the store. With this list, Tim worked industriously when no customers were at the register. When he understood exactly what his manager meant, Tim became the exemplary employee.

Tim's experience illustrates one of the remarkable assets of adolescents and young adults with AS. Once they know the expectations or rules of a situation, they are often more conscientious workers than many of their so-called typical peers. They are less likely to be disturbed by workplace gossip and politics, and they are scrupulous about doing a day's work for a day's pay.

○ Use lists, outlines, and other graphic organizers to help the adolescent remember complex directions. Even if the adolescent can recite the directions, he or she may not be able to remember the directions and follow them at the same time.

○ Model desirable communicative behavior. The adolescent with AS might not realize that it's okay for an adult to communicate in a flippant or cynical manner with her friends or colleagues but that it's not okay for the adolescent to act the same way with the same people.

- Similarly, save gossip and innuendo for times when the adolescent is definitely out of earshot. Like the two-year-old who repeats the "only" swear word that his father has ever used, adolescents with AS are likely to repeat the darnedest things.

- Our own attitude must be constructive: if we view the adolescent's behavior as a result of communicative constraint and lack of experience, we'll be able to teach, rather than judge. We'll also be able to avoid the trap of taking communicative errors too personally.

STRATEGIES TO TEACH

- In general, it's important to teach what something is not, as well as what it is. Adolescents with AS are prone to faulty assumptions about life in general and communication in particular. So, if you teach them to use a certain communicative strategy in certain places, also inform them where they should not use it.

- Act as an interpreter or translator. Find out the current slang and teach the adolescent what it means. This can save the adolescent from humiliation and future teasing. Consider this incident: Alex is an avid and talented trombone player. He has read about the great trombonists of the Jazz Age, and he has seen the instrument referred to as a 'bone. When a classmate asked Alex if he was a "boner," Alex said, "Sure." Alex was perplexed when the other boy collapsed into gales of laughter. He was even more confused when the news that "Alex said he was a boner" circulated through the middle school halls. Finally, Alex came home and asked his parents what was so funny about it. His dad explained the reference to a male body part. Embarrassed and angry, Alex demanded "Why didn't you tell me?" His father said, "I'm sorry, Alex. I just didn't know what the guys were saying."

- Although it's hard to keep up with all of the nuances of adolescent communication, we do need to teach our kids what we know to be the basics of what things mean and what not to say.

○ Teach about multiple meanings. At home and in one-to-one interactions at school, use words that can have several meanings. Demonstrate how the same word can mean different things, depending upon the context. For many adolescents, it helps to keep a "dictionary" of multiple-meaning words. When outside of these "protected waters," find a way to signal the adolescent that a word is one of those multiple-meaning words.

○ Similarly, teach figures of speech. Even older adolescents with AS have trouble interpreting figures of speech and proverbs. First teach the meaning of the expression. Then help the adolescent speculate upon why the expression has come to mean what it does. Encourage the adolescent to identify and cultivate interesting expressions. Again, however, teach them when and where they should and should not use certain expressions!

○ Help the adolescent understand and use contingent comments and questions. For example, teach the rule, "When another person introduces a topic, it's a good idea to ask them two or three follow-up questions. It's not a good idea to change the topic immediately to what you want to say."

○ Help the adolescent understand when to speak. Carol Gray's *Comic Strip Conversations* provides a nice visual example of this. In her program, each person's words are contained in bubbles. Students learn that interruptions occur when the bubbles collide. They learn to wait long enough for one person to finish her thought before they interject their own comments or questions. (The reference for *Comic Strip Conversations* can be found in the Resources section at the back of this book.)

○ Develop scripts for commonly occurring and/or problem situations. "Social stories" (again see Carol Gray's work) can be very helpful in this regard, especially if the social story contains not only the script but also the perspective on how other people feel. Some examples of social stories for adolescents can be found in the Appendix.

○ Teach the rules of swearing. My son would never swear and I'm sure yours wouldn't either, but we need to teach kids when they absolutely cannot swear. And we need to tell them not to confront other kids who break the swearing rules. Also, don't forget to teach where and when they can't use nonverbal swearing.

○ Provide guidelines about privacy and discretion. Many adolescents with AS don't recognize that certain information is private, to be shared only with immediate family or close friends. One mother made a chart of concentric circles. In the innermost circle that corresponded to immediate family, she wrote things like "How much money our family makes," "Mom's views on abortion," "Grandma's trip to the psychiatric hospital," and "My sister's bra size." In the next circle (extended family and good friends), she listed, "Our family is thinking about moving to another town," "Aunt Jane is expecting, but she isn't telling many people yet," and "Dad is interviewing for a new job." As she worked her way all the way to the outside circle (people you meet in public places), the mother helped her daughter develop the skills to be more discreet. Even though the daughter wasn't always sure exactly why a certain rule applied, she was bound and determined to follow the rule. She also relished adding new situations to the "circle chart."

○ By the way, it's important to teach about the boundaries of physical contact and display in much the same way. The concentric circle strategy works well here. Another mother developed a color sign system, using American Sign Language. When she and her daughter entered a novel or problematic situation, the mother discreetly signed a color that corresponded to certain levels of physical contact (for example, the sign for "red" means no physical contact, the sign for "yellow" means a handshake but no hug or kiss). Although most of us think about the physical contact and display issue most vividly in terms of adolescent girls, it's just as important to teach these rules to the boys as well.

○ Since most of us were in school, there has been a dramatic shift in the culture's tolerance for what might be considered "harassment" (sexual or otherwise). It's important for us to teach our kids what they absolutely cannot say or do. I teach all adolescent boys that stop means stop and no means no, to remind them that they must heed the words of others. In the beginning, we don't talk about this rule in terms of sexual harassment or date rape. We simply work on inhibition. As the boys start to become interested in girls, we extend the rule to the sexual realm. Obviously, girls need to learn the same lessons.

○ Adolescents with AS benefit from rules about adjusting one's tone of voice, body language, and choice of words for different people. They may not realize that they should stand up straight, use a polite voice, and avoid slang and swear words when talking with their grandparents. Rules such as "avoid swearing, slang, and slumping in the presence of elders, teachers, and bosses" can be quite helpful.

○ We also need to work on reading the nonverbal communication of other people and using nonverbal behavior that sends the right message. (This is more than just eye contact. In fact, professionals have been so focused on establishing eye contact for kids with AS and other communication disorders that we've neglected other areas.) Teach "survival rules" for nonverbal communication and write them down. Examples: When an adult suddenly stops talking, everyone should freeze. When a teacher shuts off the lights, everyone should freeze. When an adult gives "the look" (demonstrate this frequently), be quiet and listen. Don't touch someone unless they say it's okay.

○ Another way to work on nonverbal communication is to use developmentally appropriate movies on video. Turn off the sound and watch a scene. Then talk about what the characters were "saying." How did we know, when we couldn't hear the words? Write down your ideas. Then turn on the sound but turn away from the video. What do we understand when we just hear the words? Again, write down your ideas. Finally, watch the scene again, with both sound and visual information. How does our interpretation change when we can put it all together? Once the adolescent learns to do this with videos, you can begin "real life" interpretation. This can occur in skits or role playing in the speech pathologist's or counselor's office. Students may choose to perform skits for classmates during health class or Family and Consumer Science. Finally, you can debrief about actual interactions, taking care to emphasize that this kind of debriefing should occur out of earshot of the involved parties.

○ Work on voice volume and intonation. Rules may help: Don't use a loud voice in the school library. Signals can help: "Confidential voice" or a hand signal that conveys the same thing. Role playing and reading aloud are also helpful tools. Some adolescents with AS even enjoy participating in the drama club. By working on "being in character" they achieve greater command over their voice and their body language.

○ Devise rules about personal space. Many adolescents with AS learned about their "personal bubble" in elementary school. Some of them are even able to carry this concept into adolescence. But the rules of personal space do change somewhat in middle and high school, since everyone tends to have tenuous control over his or her body. We need to teach our adolescents a rule of thumb that keeps them from intruding on others. And we also need to teach them a socially appropriate response for those occasions when they feel intruded upon (in other words, not to scream "Ow! You entered my bubble!").

○ We need to help our adolescents master ways to clarify confusion. If they don't understand what someone means, how can they politely ask for clarification?

○ Come up with developmentally appropriate ways of asking for help. Even though whining is not considered a "cool" strategy in middle school, it may be the only way the student knows to get help. It's important to help him or her find an easy but acceptable way of seeking assistance.

A FINAL NOTE

Often it's frustrating for parents and teachers to realize that the adolescent with AS can follow the rules without understanding the principles. Parents sometimes say, "But I want her to understand being respectful to authority figures." Teachers may remark, "He's doing it from the script. It's not really him."

My answer to both is this: They'll get there eventually. In the meantime, we have to equip them with the communicative behaviors that will allow them to interact with others. The principles will become more clear to them when they have many opportunities to practice communication.

A FINAL, FINAL NOTE

Communication is the essence of being human. But it isn't serious all the time. In fact, most of us learn best through warmth and humor. Keeping our sense of humor and cultivating our children's humor is a terrific coping strategy for all. It also cements our working partnership and makes our journey through life more fun.

Oh, and when a peer asks the adolescent girl what she thinks of what Christina and Jenna were saying, she can always fall back on that adolescent Script of Scripts: "whatever."

And—don't forget—you can't *not* communicate.

CHAPTER FOUR

Memory, Organization, and the "Executive Functions"

Janine Thompson is a seventeen-year-old high school junior. She is most comfortable when her life is predictable and organized. Janine always has perfectly manicured nails, flawless makeup, and "not a hair out of place." This is all the more remarkable since Janine's school bus comes at 6:15 every morning! Janine manages by having a morning routine that is timed to the minute. It includes time for showering, drying and curling her hair, dressing in clothes ironed the night before, and eating the same breakfast every school morning. Since Janine knows exactly how long it takes to get ready to go in the morning, she also can adjust her alarm clock to give her ample getting-ready time on days when she doesn't have school.

Last week, Janine and her mother were supposed to visit her aunt on a day off from school. They had arranged to meet the aunt for shopping at 9:30. Janine's mother told Janine that they would need to leave the house at 8:45. Janine set her alarm and got up early enough to do her morning routine. About an hour before they were supposed to leave, Janine's aunt called. Could they move their meeting time up to 9:15? Janine's mother agreed and then went to tell Janine. "You said what?" Janine cried. "That's impossible! I can't get ready fifteen minutes earlier!"

Always a calm person, Mrs. Thompson matter of factly reassured Janine that she could, indeed, get ready in time. "And if you don't have time to eat cereal, I'll make you a bagel and cream cheese for the road."

Janine lost it. She began to cry and scream, "I can't. I can't." Mrs. Thompson was baffled. She hadn't seen Janine that upset in years. Was her daughter under some pressure that she didn't know about?

Mrs. Thompson called her sister and said that they wouldn't be able to meet that early. They arranged a rain check. Then Mrs. Thompson went back to Janine, who was still storming around the house. Fortunately, Mrs. Thompson knew about LOW and SLOW, so she just sat in the room with Janine for a while and didn't try to offer advice.

After about 45 minutes, Janine began to settle down. "I can't change my schedule," she finally said. "If I don't have time to do everything on the list, I'm sunk. I don't know what I can leave out."

Mrs. Thompson realized that what she had labeled Janine's "rigidity" was actually her way of keeping organized. As a younger child, Janine had been scattered. The family had helped Janine develop routines that she could memorize. What no one understood was that Janine didn't have a "Plan B." If "Plan A" couldn't work, Janine didn't have a set of strategies to put in its place. Janine's "rigidity" was the only way she knew to cope with her own disorganization and confusion.

Janine's difficulties demonstrate one of the most frustrating aspects of being an adolescent with Asperger Syndrome. Needless to say, this is also one of the most frustrating aspects of being the parent or teacher of an individual with AS. In spite of knowledge and skills in many areas, adolescents with AS can be remarkably incompetent in using their abilities in everyday life.

Nancy Minshew, a researcher and clinician in Pittsburgh, has suggested that the autism spectrum disorders (like AS) reflect the inability to be flexible, adaptive, and social in everyday life. For the adolescent with AS, difficulties in flexibility, adaptability, and socialization emerge in part from inefficient memory, organization, and "executive functions."

WHAT DO YOU MEAN . . . INEFFICIENT MEMORY?

You're right. Your child can probably remember what he had for dinner at the family's favorite restaurant on March 24, 1995. Or she can remember the evolution of each Pokémon character. Or perhaps the call letters of all NBC affiliates west of the Mississippi. Or even more impressively, the capitals of all of the countries in Africa.

In fact, children and adolescents with AS usually don't have any trouble remembering factual data or information stored in their rote memory. They are particularly skilled in recalling information when they have topic control. For some adolescents with AS, recall of information depends on being able to say everything about the topic from start to finish. But for most, recall of even isolated pieces of information is deceptively simple.

Most adolescents with AS are also quite skilled in remembering routines. Once the routine is established, they seldom forget a step. In fact, they may protest when you leave out a step. No experience illustrates this better than cooking with an adolescent with AS who has just taken "Foods" in school. He or she will argue to the death upon seeing the shortcuts that most of us non-food-professionals take in the kitchen! "What do you mean it doesn't matter if you sift the flour five times? The recipe says five times! My foods teacher said five times!"

So, where are these so-called memory problems?

WORKING MEMORY

Working memory is a short-term memory store that allows us to hold onto pieces of information while performing mental operations on that information. Mental arithmetic is the most obvious example of this. Remembering what you went upstairs to get, while simultaneously picking up all the junk on the steps, is another example (unfortunately, an example that most of us fail at, after the age of 40 or so). For adolescents, working memory is also necessary for "holding onto" the safety precautions for science lab while mixing your chemicals, in remembering all the points you want to make in your social studies essay question, and for holding onto your idea while your friend talks on and on about her new sweater. Adolescents with AS can really get lost in working memory—perhaps because their self-regulatory inefficiencies interfere with their ability to pay attention to the information to begin with, perhaps because their communicative challenges keep them from understanding what the other person means or perhaps because of an actual memory defect. Regardless of the reasons, the glitches in working memory can truly interfere with the adolescent's ability to show what she knows "on demand." As you'll learn below, we can make a number of fairly simple modifications and teach some "survival strategies" that can make a huge difference in this area.

REMEMBERING TO REMEMBER

Children and adolescents with AS also **"forget to remember."** In other words, they often don't realize that they have information, skills, or strategies that might help them with a certain problem. They don't make the connection between the current situation and previous ones that were similar. It's as if each problem were brand new. One reason for this may be the difficulty in inhibition. If you don't inhibit or stop yourself before acting, you don't have time to reflect on the problem at hand. You don't have time to think about your prior experience and to use hindsight or forethought. Another problem with "remembering to remember" may be the way in which memories were stored in the first place. For many people with AS, each event or set of facts is stored as though it had its own little compartment. There may not be many connecting ties

Temple Grandin, Ph. D., an expert on animal science and livestock feeding and handling—and also an adult with "high-functioning autism" (HFA)—tells about learning about dogs. As a child and adolescent, she knew what a German Shepherd looked like and what a Pekingese was. She knew Great Danes and miniature poodles. In her mind's eye, she had a picture for each breed. What she couldn't form was a generic image of "dog." What was it, she said, that made a dog a dog?

Dr. Grandin's story illustrates what happens with many individuals with AS or HFA: Their memories are stored in highly specific ways without the conceptual bridges that might link them together efficiently.

between these compartmentalized memories. Thus, a new problem may indeed seem unlike anything ever encountered before.

Another problem with "remembering to remember" may be one of retrieval. The adolescent knows that she knows something relevant, but she simply can't find the information. Without the conceptual links mentioned above, memories are stored in the brain's equivalent of the piles of papers under my desk. Without the nervous system equivalent of file folders, it's hard to get to the information in a timely way. Not surprisingly, productivity declines and opportunities are lost when these retrieval problems occur.

Finally, some individuals with AS have inefficient declarative or representational memory. This is the aspect of memory that allows us to be creative—to remember experiences and information from several sources and to put it together to tell something, like the story of our life. It also helps us reconstruct, when our rote memory fails. For example, when the high school sophomore doesn't remember the textbook definition for "pedestrian," she can think about other words that sound similar. Her thinking might be: "How about 'equestrian'? That's someone who rides a horse. Maybe '-estrian' has something to do with traveling. If equestrian is someone who travels on a horse, what does a pedestrian travel on? Oh, my mom wears these silly socks called Peds under her shoes. Maybe 'ped' means foot. Oh, yeah, now I remember my French word 'pied.' I guess that a pedestrian is someone who travels on foot." In a typically developing adolescent, this reasoning progresses in a flash, much faster than the time it took you to read it. But in students with AS, such reconstruction is often slow and clumsy. We'll talk more about this in Chapter Five, "Thinking and Learning."

AND WHAT ARE THESE "EXECUTIVE FUNCTIONS"?

Simply put, executive functions are what an executive does. In a corporation, the executive analyzes a situation and makes a plan. She allocates the resources. She gets the job going, either directly or through people who work for her. She monitors production, making sure that the original plan makes sense. She redirects workers when they get off track. If the plan isn't working, she modifies the plan and shifts strategy. She knows when the project is finished. In other words, the executive's function is to manage every step in getting the product to market.

When psychologists and educators first started talking about the executive functions, we assumed that they were mental processes that emerged in late childhood and early adolescence. Hence the beginnings of major school projects in fourth and fifth grades.

Now we know that we can see the buds of executive functions in toddlers. Whenever the eighteen-month-old toddles across the room toward a fascinating object and looks back at his parent for a reaction, executive functions are operating. That split-second inhibition and the (sometime) shift in behavior—the pause between impulse and action—are the beginnings of executive functions!

Unfortunately, it's not quite that simple for adolescents in general and even harder for adolescents with AS. As you know from Chapter Two, the regulation of the Four A's is often difficult for adolescents with AS. It's hard to make a plan if your insides are screaming with noise overload or if you're so aroused that your attention is darting from one thing to another. And, as you can imagine after reading about communication, it's practically impossible to sustain effort and inhibit distraction if you didn't quite comprehend what your mother wanted you to do in the first place. To add further load to the overload, it's hard to carry through with even the best of plans if you can't remember what you planned to do! No wonder individuals with AS have the reputation of doing the same routines over and over. If it works, why change it?

I've also run into another stumbling block for the organizational and executive skills of adolescents with AS. We can call it the "Why does it matter?" phenomenon. Let's face it, a fair amount of what we do in life may not end up mattering in the objective grand scheme of things. (I put making beds in this category, but you may have a different view.) Most of our children share this "Oh, there she goes again" interpretation of parent and teacher preferences. Kids with fairly decent organizational skills and a strong desire to please (if only to butter us up for a privilege later on), will do what we ask just because we said so. This often doesn't work for adolescents with AS, however. First, their organizational skills probably aren't fairly decent to begin with, and they have to conserve their resources for the really important stuff. Second, they often don't see the value of doing something "just because." In fact, in twenty-something years of working with kids, I've rarely if ever convinced an adolescent with AS that he or she should do something to "butter up" an adult. "What does getting on her good side have to do with it?" they want to know. This is in contrast to their ADHD "cousins," who are equally or more disorganized, but who quickly grasp the concept of "catching more flies with honey than with vinegar." In the long run, the impetus for adolescents with AS usually resides in finding ways to free up more time for the things that really matter to them.

Finally, as illustrated by Janine's story above, we have to recognize that once the adolescent with AS does come upon a problem-solving strategy, it can be carved in stone. Like Mrs. Thompson, though, we have to remember that this "rigidity" or "insistence upon sameness" reflects in part the difficulty in responding spontaneously to life's dilemmas. When we're creating the rules and strategies to help the adolescent organize, we have to build in flexibility. Or as the saying goes, "Never say never . . . "

SO, HOW CAN WE HELP?

Before we help, we have to gain the adolescent's interest in becoming more efficient. While it's logical to us that anyone would want to get "more bang for the buck," our adolescents might not be convinced. I often go back to: "These ideas might help you finish your work sooner. That leaves more time for _____."

This may sound like a broken record, but we also have to ensure that the regulatory foundation is in place before we can expect memory and executive functions to work efficiently. Please check back with Chapter Two if you've forgotten these strategies.

It's equally important that the adolescent understand what we mean for him or her to do. Many executive wild-goose chases occur because the person doing the planning didn't understand the true nature of the problem. Providing the communicative supports is one way to avoid wild-goose chases.

As when helping with self-regulation or communication, our approach to memory and executive function glitches involves a combination of modifications of the environment (including our behavior) and direct teaching of skills. And, as stated in past chapters, no one strategy works for everyone. That said, here are some ideas that have worked for others.

MODIFICATIONS OF THE ENVIRONMENT (INCLUDING OUR BEHAVIOR)

THE PURPOSE OF THE TASK

○ Carefully analyze each task to determine its purpose. Once you've determined the purpose, eliminate any function that isn't directly related to the purpose. For example, if you want to ensure that the student knows the precise meanings of vocabulary words, provide word banks instead of requiring him to recall all the potential word matches. If you want to ensure that the student knows and applies the formulas for perimeter and area of various geometric figures, let her show the formula but then do the computation on the calculator. At home, if your goal is to ensure that he has showered, brushed, flossed, and applied deodorant, put a list on the wall beside the sink (at eye level!) rather than requiring him to "just know."

○ In general, give up on the expectation that they should "just know." If they did, I wouldn't be writing this book. And if they don't just know, it's not because we failed in our roles as parents, teachers, or psychologists!

○ Always convey the purpose of the task to the adolescent. If the assignment is a rough draft, remind him that this is a version to get his ideas on paper and spelling and handwriting don't matter. On the other hand, if this is the final edit, she needs to use spell check *and* read it over carefully.

MAKING CONNECTIONS

○ Use concept maps, Venn diagrams, and other graphic organizers as you teach. (This will actually help all of the

students, not just those with AS and other executive function inefficiencies.) Using these will help the student draw
the connections between and among facts, concepts, and
events. Using these will also help you remember to emphasize those connections. (We all need a little organizational
assistance every once in a while!) If you don't have ready
access to a library of graphic organizers, see the LINKS and
Inspiration references in the Resources section.

○ For students with poor handwriting or copying skills, provide graphic organizers with critical information already
filled in. Again, do you want the student to learn the concepts, or do you want him to practice writing neatly in
tiny boxes?

NOTE TAKING

○ And that leads us to taking notes in class. Note taking is a
nightmare for adolescents with AS or other learning/com-
munication disorders. For many, the monsters include
handwriting difficulties, especially when writing quickly.
Even copying is problematic for many students. In fact,
research has suggested that for some students the brain
power expended in copying can interfere with learning.
Aside from the writing/copying issue, note taking for students with AS becomes overwhelming because of their
attentional and communication difficulties. As we said
above, it's often difficult for them to discern the most
important elements of what someone is saying and to
inhibit their reactions to "off task" stimulation. They often
attempt to compensate by trying to write down everything
the teacher says. Then they become so mired down in
remembering and writing what was said that they don't
have brainpower left over for understanding.

The Bottom Line: Give them the notes and a high-
lighter. They can follow along and highlight what you tell
them is important. They'll be able to listen and to think
about what you're saying. Relax, though—we will teach
them to take notes (see Direct Teaching, below). It will just
be in a way that matches their brains.

ORGANIZING TASKS

○ Find a way of recording assignments that fits with the student's strengths and challenges. Be prepared for resistance— writing down assignments is one of those things that "doesn't matter" in the minds of most adolescents (with or without AS). As with note taking, we'll teach them a way to do it on their own, eventually. For the time being, though, think of providing weekly or online assignment sheets or a syllabus as in college courses.

○ If an event is coming up in the future (such as a project or test), list it on every day's assignment sheet. Adolescents with AS are very literal; they may not remember that they need to study or work on a long-term project unless it's listed.

○ At school and at home, model calendar keeping, list making, and other memory-enhancing strategies. In my office, I routinely and obviously go to my Day-Timer and write down things that I'm supposed to remember for my adolescent clients. In the beginning, they're surprised. "Can't you remember anything?" they ask. "I just want to make sure I remember. Sometimes I get so caught up in thinking about other things that I forget something important," I assure them. Many of my adolescents now say before they leave,

---

One day I sat in a meeting in which seventh-grade teachers bemoaned a student's inability to write down and turn in homework assignments. The student is exceptionally bright, so the teachers were understandably frustrated with his inefficiency regarding homework. The student had told me that he couldn't write down the assignment because he was too busy packing up his books to move to the next class (an anxiety-provoking task for him). In the meeting, I asked the teachers if they could write the homework assignment on the board at the beginning of class. "That won't work," said one. "I never know what I'm going to assign until the end of class."

As she later confessed, the student wasn't the only one with organizational challenges! She decided that giving all of the students a weekly assignment sheet would help her keep on track! After that, my seventh grader and most of his friends were much more efficient. ※

"Now check to make sure you have my appointment written down for next time."

PERSISTING AND INHIBITING

○ Provide a role model for sustaining effort and inhibiting
   irrelevant reactions. I'll never forget my first statistics class
   in graduate school. As the days of September waned, we
   heard less and less about statistics and more and more
   about the Red Sox. I was somewhat perplexed by the view
   that one could live and die by the fortunes of nine guys in
   baseball uniforms and red socks. It seemed that every "statistical measure of central tendency" led to a story about a
   Red Sox tragedy. Now I know that such single-mindedness
   is not just a function of AS but also a function of being a
   long-suffering Red Sox fan. But, I also remember thinking, "He won't be so forgiving if we digress in our essays
   on the unit test!" The moral of the story: If we want our
   kids to stay on track, we need to stay on track ourselves.
   Particularly for students with AS and other learning disorders, once off track it's hard to get back on.

○ At home, it's equally important to support the adolescent's
   organizational efforts. If he wants to write a list to make
   sure he doesn't forget any detail of cleaning his room,
   then let him (it's not just his attempt to avoid "the
   inevitable"). If she is in midstream of a task, try not to
   interrupt unless the situation is the equivalent of impend-
   ing disaster. Again, once derailed, it's hard for them to get
   back on track.

○ Use task cards to support working memory and executive
   functions. As mentioned in Chapter Two, examples of these
   can be found in the Appendix.

○ Help the adolescent break large tasks down into smaller
   chunks. Agree that different chunks can be done at different times. For example, who decreed that the entire room
   has to be cleaned on Saturday morning? What if she picks
   up all the dirty clothes and puts them in the hamper every
   day? Then vacuuming can be reserved for Sunday evening

(to clear the debris from all the weekend fun and to start the week off right).

○ Respect the adolescent's increasing awareness of his/her own arousal/alertness levels. If he insists that social studies questions can be done most easily while sitting on the living room couch covered with an afghan and listening to Mozart or *Rubber Soul*, go with it! At least until results prove otherwise. Similarly, if math comes easier in the morning before school than in the afternoon, help her get up a little earlier.

THE WORKING PARTNERSHIP

○ Cultivate a problem-solving relationship with your adolescent. When things don't seem to be going right, approach her with words like, "I've noticed that you're having to work later and later at night. Can we talk about what would help you be more efficient, so you can have some free time occasionally?" In the beginning, it may be hard for your adolescent to generate alternatives. If you model and practice brainstorming and objective evaluation of possible solutions, it's likely that you'll eventually be surprised by your child's creativity.

STRATEGIES TO TEACH YOUR ADOLESCENT

"SELF-AFFIRMATIONS"

○ "It's not you. You're not lazy or stupid. You have many strengths. But you are inefficient in some ways." It's amazing how helpful it is for adolescents to realize, "It's not me, it's my brain." Used as a mantra, this can help them when their confidence is flagging.

○ "It's not a sign of weakness or stupidity to use lists, assignment sheets, or graphic organizers. Everybody learns differently." Another mantra. This can help adolescents who resist modifications because they're self-conscious about being different.

MNEMONICS

○ Teach memory strategies (or mnemonics, as your adolescent will inform you). Many adolescents don't automatically put information together in meaningful chunks. Try an assignment like this: "Sally has to buy supplies for the class cookout. She needs mustard, straws, hamburger buns, soda, napkins, pickle relish, hamburger, plastic cups, silverware, hot dogs, ketchup, chips, hot dog rolls, and paper plates. Think of two different ways Sally could organize her list to make it easier to remember." HINT: Some of us do better with a location-based list (What items are on which aisles in the store?), while some of us work better with semantic categories (What goes with hamburgers? What paper/plastic goods do I need?). Once your adolescent learns a couple of mnemonic strategies, you can begin to talk about which strategy is best for each type of task or for each type of brain.

○ Teach the adolescent to write down information that is easy to forget. For example, if she's listening to a friend give directions to her house, write down the names of streets, turns, or landmarks.

○ Help the adolescent understand which type of directions works best for him or her (this is especially important for new and not-so-new drivers). Does a map work better? Or does he do better with written directions? (Go three miles and then turn left at the Shell station.)

PLAN A, PLAN B, PLAN C . . .

○ Teach routines for commonly occurring tasks or activities. Don't forget to write them down (or have the adolescent do so). Common routines include: before bed routine (including packing the backpack and getting out clothes for the next day); morning routine; after school routine, specific to each day of the week; and household chores and responsibilities.

○ For each routine, teach your adolescent to make a Plan B for the zigger zagger days (see Chapter Two if you've forgotten zigger zaggers). For example, if he oversleeps and doesn't have time to eat two bowls of cereal, he can toast a bagel, load on cream cheese and jelly, and take it to go. Or, if she doesn't have time to iron her clothes for tomorrow, she can wear something that doesn't show wrinkles. Don't forget to reassure them that we all have bad hair days every once in a while.

CONCEPTS AND ORGANIZATION

- ○ Help the students learn to understand what their graphic organizers really mean. For example, if a "central concept" uniting all of the New England colonies was "the desire for religious freedom," that means that all of the colonies began because people wanted to achieve that goal. If we don't help the students understand these ideas from a "general to specific" and a "specific to general" perspective, they're at risk for just memorizing the graphic organizer. In fact, this is a risk for many adolescents, with or without AS.
- ○ Teach adolescents to use outlines, graphic organizers, and paragraph templates to organize their own ideas. We'll talk more about this in Chapter Five, "Thinking and Learning."

SELF-MANAGEMENT

- ○ Once a task or assignment is broken into chunks, help the adolescent learn to self-monitor and self-reinforce. Let's say that she is writing an essay using the "five-paragraph essay template." In the middle of the second paragraph, she has a craving for a cookie. Instead of going to the kitchen right away, she looks at where she is in the template and makes a deal with herself: "I'll go at the end of this paragraph." As she goes in search of the cookie, she can congratulate herself for getting to a good stopping place. Maybe (if we're really lucky) she'll even start to think about paragraph three as she munches.
- ○ Have the student keep a notebook or filebox of helpful strategies. When an assignment or task comes around, he can look in the filebox for helpful hints.

ASSIGNMENT BOOKS AND NOTE TAKING

○ Creating an assignment book—for most adolescents, this is an onerous task. Perhaps the hardest part is selling this as a wise thing to spend time on. For some kids, it does help to remind them that this will give them more free time in the long run. When all else fails, I suggest that it's not worth it to lose "brownie points" for something as easy as assignment recording. I tell the adolescent I'd rather see them save their brownie points for the stuff that's really worth it. Start at the level where the adolescent is currently most consistent, no matter how simple that may seem. For example, if the adolescent is not yet recording any assignments, start by having him or her go to the team's "master" assignment page and photocopy the entire sheet (or print the page from an online assignment log). Once this is mastered, you may have the student be responsible for recording the assignment for one class (start with the most straightforward one) and having it initialed by the teacher.

○ Teach a systematic strategy for note taking. There are several different systems illustrated in *LINKS*, in *Teach Me Language*, and in commercially available study skills books.

Some students with AS do well with a two-column approach (see example on the next page). Key terms are listed in the left column, and critical points are "bulleted" in the right column. This (or any) approach can be taught in a step-by-step manner. For example, begin by providing two-column notes for the student. Initially the student's job is to highlight elements in the right-hand column that are particularly important. After she masters this, provide only the terms in the left column and require her to fill in critical points on the right. With this skill firmly established, the student can then follow the approach independently.

It doesn't matter which note-taking approach you teach, as long as it fits the student's learning style. In fact, these strategies usually work best when the adolescent takes some ownership of what works best for his or her brain. For example, some students with AS find it quite helpful to

EXAMPLE OF TWO-COLUMN NOTE TAKING

TOPIC <u>HEAT TRANSFER</u>   PAGES <u>49–50</u>

Term	Key Points
Heat Transfer	• The movement of energy from a warmer object to a cooler object
Conduction	• Heat transfer by direct contact of particles of matter
Convection	• Heat transfer by the movement of a heated fluid
Convection current	• The flow that transfers heat within a fluid
	• Caused by heating and cooling of the fluid, changes in the fluid's density, and gravity
Convection cell	• One complete loop of a convection current
Importance of	• Heat transfer has affected the mantle
heat transfer	and crust of the earth
	• Changes in the heat and density of the mantle can cause shifts in land masses (continents)

include drawings or comments about personal experiences as aids to their recall.

Don't forget, though, that we can't stop providing notes for the student until she can take notes automatically and independently under the load of classroom conditions. The fact that someone says she's supposed to be able to take notes in high school (or college) doesn't mean that she'll be ready to do it easily at that magic time. Our purpose must remain twofold here—teaching a study skill, while at the same time providing the support that our adolescent needs to master course material.

A FINAL NOTE

Once Janine developed a Plan B for her morning routine and for other areas in which others considered her "rigid," she was able to be much more flexible and adaptable. Plan B even became a code around the Thompson household, used for feedback to all family members when they were getting a little inflexible.

Like self-regulation and communication, attention and the executive functions are processes that most of us struggle with throughout our lifetimes. They are extremely sensitive to stress and developmental change. Hence, the Plan A that worked for us as single adults is unlikely to work for us as working parents.

When I was an adolescent, my father told the story of his college psychology professor. This gentleman told his students that, in psychology, the test questions always stayed the same from year to year. It was just the answers that changed.

Isn't that the story of life? For our adolescents, we have to build the attentional, memory, and executive functions that hold up in a world of changing answers.

CHAPTER FIVE

Thinking and Learning

Ralph was a high school junior when his parents brought him to psychotherapy. Ralph had always struggled academically. Although he seemed to be bright in many areas, he just wasn't able to show his knowledge in standard ways. His parents understood this and assumed that Ralph would find his niche in adulthood. They sought psychotherapy for Ralph because of social issues. Apparently, Ralph was considered rather unusual by his classmates. When high school life didn't go as he expected, Ralph began to "talk funny." While his parents and teachers were concerned about the reactions of his peers, they also were relieved that all Ralph was doing was talking. When he was younger, Ralph had hit others when he was frustrated. "Talking funny" was something of an improvement! His classmates didn't understand this, though.

One of the first things the psychologist asked Ralph was what he was saying when others thought he was talking funny. "Oh, I'm just responding to them in Arabic. Then I can say what I really feel without other people knowing." Ralph's psychologist was taken aback, wondering if the young man had delusions of knowing Arabic. How could a seventeen-year-old in a small town in the heartland of America know Arabic? When the psychologist asked Ralph's parents about this, they replied that Ralph certainly could know

Arabic. Dr. Jones, Ralph's father, was an archaeologist who had worked in Egypt when Ralph was younger. Ralph had enjoyed sitting around with the workers on the dig. Maybe the "funny talk" really was Arabic.

When the adults brought Ralph into the session, Dr. Jones asked him a question in Arabic. Ralph replied immediately, in what Dr. Jones identified as flawless Arabic. The psychologist then asked Ralph if he knew other languages. "Oh, yes. I'm fluent in Spanish and French. I also know a little Hebrew, from the time we were in Jerusalem." No one had taught Ralph these languages. He just learned them by listening to others and talking to the workers and household help.

Dr. Jones then asked his son what he was saying at school. It turned out that Ralph wasn't "talking funny." He was just "using his words" the ones he had picked up on the family's travels around the world.

Over the years that the psychologist worked with him, Ralph continued to use his words in a variety of situations that confused or distressed him. He often wrote lengthy accounts of interactions with others or composed short stories. In each of these, he wrote certain parts (usually the upsetting parts) in another language. (At the psychologist's request, he also provided translations in parentheses.) It was clear that Ralph was using a unique intellectual skill to manage the parts of his life that he was less skilled in understanding.

By the way, once the folks at school knew that Ralph wasn't talking funny, but just talking in another language, they relaxed somewhat. In fact, many of his peers became intrigued with his knowledge of other cultures and with his stories of worldwide travel. Kids being kids, they also asked him to teach them swear words in other languages. Ralph's parents and psychologist had to coach him on when and where to provide such translations, and he generally adhered to these rules. The final outcome was that this "special skill" allowed Ralph to end his high school years with some sense of connection to his peers. In addition, it demonstrated to the faculty that their assumptions about Ralph as an unmotivated and odd student were unfounded.

This chapter is about how adolescents with Asperger Syndrome think and learn. Thinking and learning are aspects of "cognitive development"—our growing ability to "know."

The cognitive skills of adolescents with AS are just as variable as they skills of their peers without AS. Just like "typically developing" adolescents, some are extremely bright and others are less so. The diagnosis of AS does presume at least average intellectual ability, but within that range are many combinations of strengths and challenges.

Even though no one adolescent with AS fits a mold perfectly, some common themes arise. The vignette about Ralph demonstrates some of the characteristics of how adolescents with AS think and learn:

- As younger children, students with AS may have developed particular interests or passions. These may continue into adolescence or may be replaced by new areas of interest.
- While the areas of interest may seem odd initially, there is usually a connection between the interest and a specific experience.
- The adolescent's fund of information regarding selected topics can be remarkably deep and broad.
- Once interested in a topic, the adolescent with AS may devote a great deal of time and energy to learning more.
- Even within the area of interest, knowledge often is literal or fact-based. Applying knowledge to novel situations or making inferences may be difficult. In other words, knowing "what" is easier than knowing "how," for the adolescent with AS.
- Special skills can coexist with clear-cut gaps in cognitive functioning.
- Once the adolescent establishes a certain way of thinking about a topic, it may be hard for him or her to shift to another interpretation.
- "Missing the forest for the trees" is another relatively common cognitive glitch.
- What the adolescent knows may be very different from what he or she shows "on demand."

In the pages that follow, we'll talk about how these (and other) characteristics can help and hinder students with AS as they journey through life. Just remember, it's rare for any adolescent to exhibit all of these characteristics. As cautioned in previous chapters, it's important to know each child's specific strengths and vulnerabilities if we are to provide assistance that works!

In her presentations, Dr. Temple Grandin used to show a slide of the National Aeronautics and Space Administration (NASA) building. Dr. Grandin would then comment, "Here is the NASA lab. Also known as a sheltered workshop for adults with Asperger Syndrome and high-functioning autism." As an individual who identifies herself as a person with autism, Dr. Grandin is able to poke fun at the particular strengths of others with similar challenges. She is also quick to poke fun at the rest of the world—"If someone found a cure for autism, everybody would just be standing around chatting all the time. Nothing would ever get done!"

While life is never as simple as jokes, it seems that many individuals with AS (and high-functioning autism) possess intellectual skills that equip them for solving the scientific and mathematical questions of life. All it takes to understand this is a reframing of the characteristics that we often consider "symptoms" of AS. "Perseveration," or repetitive thoughts and actions, certainly can lead to dogged pursuit of a solution to a problem. "Inability to see the big picture" can allow the person to focus on the details that may lead to solutions. "Preference for aloneness" allows the individual to spend long hours in the lab or at the computer, far from the temptation of chatting. Although it's hard to diagnose historical figures, there are some suggestions that a number of famous scientists, inventors, and mathematicians had at least a touch of AS.

PASSIONS AND SPECIAL INTERESTS

As the old song says, "Love makes the world go 'round." And not just romantic love. We all learn the most about the things that interest us. Our passions can determine what we read, what we listen to, and where we go. Our passions affect whom we choose as friends and associates and what we pick as our life's work. So, in these ways, adolescents with AS are essentially no different from the rest of us.

In Chapter Six, we'll talk about the passions and preoccupations of adolescents with AS as they affect social and emotional development. For now, let's consider the cognitive benefits and drawbacks of "an encompassing preoccupation with one or more stereotyped and restricted patterns of interest" (one of the DSM-IV requirements for a diagnosis of AS).

The beauty of a preoccupation is that it makes us thirsty for knowledge and skill. For example, this thirst can translate into improving one's reading skills in order to understand what the encyclopedia says about the topic. It can evolve into improved research skills (on the Internet and elsewhere) as the student searches for more information. When one thing leads to another, it can help the student broaden his or her perspective about the topic itself and about life in general. Preoccupation can also lead to improved communication skills as the student seeks out the expertise of others. Mastery of a topic can lead the student to have more faith in himself or herself as a learner. Therefore, for adolescents with or without AS, preoccupations can enhance knowledge, skills, and self-esteem.

The drawbacks of passions and preoccupations occur when they interfere with other aspects of life. Like any obsession, a preoccupation with a certain topic can prevent the student from being available for learning about other things. Thirteen-year-old Walter is fascinated with the stock market. He watches CNN daily, reads the stock market pages obsessively, and spends hours online looking up quotes on the after-hours trading of various stocks. He knows the ticker-tape symbols for countless corporations and the meaning of statistics such as the "price/earnings ratio." All of this works fine until his teachers ask him to put away the stock pages in order to read his language arts assignment, or until his mother reminds him that he's spent so much time on Wall Street that he hasn't started his homework. Walter insists that he shouldn't have to learn any of that school stuff. He doesn't see its relevance to his everyday or future life. While we've made some inroads by using stock prices to teach Walter about fractions and decimals, there are functional skills that simply can't be taught in the context of Wall Street.

SO, HOW CAN WE HELP?

The rule of thumb in dealing with passions and preoccupations as they relate to thinking and learning is this: "Use the passion as an entry point, but then begin to expand."

- ○ Once an adolescent reveals a particular interest or skill, try to determine what he or she knows and why the topic/skill is so fascinating. This can be tricky, because many adolescents with AS don't reveal the full range of their knowledge on demand. We have to listen carefully to what they say spontaneously. We have to watch what they read and do when we're not "bossing them around." For most parents, the answers to questions like "What interests him?" are pretty obvious. It's the "why" that's a little more elusive.

- ○ Once we know what the adolescent knows and loves, we can begin to think "outside the box" about how to use this information. What does he or she need to know/do? How can we use the passion to get there? Sometimes, it's as obvious as using the stock market page to teach about fractions. At other times, we have to be more creative and/or tolerant. For example, Walter, our budding Wall Street wizard, balked at any work that was not directly tied to his "business." Yet he showed significant gaps in his reading comprehension, gaps that could not be bridged by merely reading the business pages. His teachers set up a "class store" for all of the students, allowing them to earn "bucks" for completed work. When allowed to buy *USA Today* at his class store every afternoon, Walter was able to devote the time and effort necessary to complete his reading and language arts assignments. This program was a major pain for the teachers, as they had to shop several times a week for the class store. They learned, however, that time spent shopping was a lot more pleasant than time spent arguing with Walter about reading assignments.

- ○ As the adolescent acquires more skills in areas outside his preoccupation, we are often able to fade out the connections with the preoccupation. This is an important step, because "real life" requires all of us to do things that we don't enjoy. As we fade out these connections, though, it's important to maintain a high level of reinforcement for the student's use of adaptive and flexible thinking and problem solving. This reinforces the adolescent's belief in him- or herself as a learner.

○ When introducing a new or difficult skill, we may have to go back to the preoccupation briefly. If nothing else, this helps us "sell" the new material as something worth learning.

○ If we know why a given topic is so intriguing, we can also introduce new topics that share common characteristics. For example, Matthew was a Beatles fan. He liked their lyrics and their musical techniques. He knew every word of every song. He knew who wrote the songs, who played what instruments, and what record company recorded each album. Matthew would talk about the Beatles with anyone who would listen. Since most of the interested listeners were over forty, Matthew's mother decided she needed to help him branch out. She began by taking him to a concert by a Beatles cover band. Once Matthew learned that he liked rock concerts, his mother got him to agree to go to a hip-hop concert. He soon became intrigued with hip-hop lyrics. He was able to talk with his peers about favorite bands and songs. While his heart still remained true to the Beatles, he had found a way of expanding his interest to match that of his peers. (By the way, Matthew also used his musical interest to support a term paper on the role of music in the social change of the 1960s and 1970s and a math project based on an imaginary record/CD company.)

○ Finally, remember that adolescents with AS may not automatically make connections between new and old material or between novel information and their interests. We often need to remind them of these connections— "Remember how we learned about fractions last month? Well, decimals are just another way of saying the same thing. Look, even the stock pages are changing over from fractions to decimals!"

LITERAL THINKING AND PROBLEMS IN "CENTRAL COHERENCE"

Parents often comment that their adolescent with AS "just doesn't get it." "It" usually refers to the gist of the information or task at hand. Adolescents with AS who miss the point of conversations are at risk for missing the point in academic and other learning situations. Some of their difficulty arises from the tendency to take everything quite literally. Another component of "getting it" is the ability to make inferences about what something is about. The latter aspect of thinking is called "central coherence"—how things hang together around a certain theme or point.

Some adolescents with AS think literally because their understanding of language is so concrete. Janine, the adolescent whose morning routine was disrupted in Chapter Four, usually gave nearly perfect definitions of her vocabulary words. She also was able to recite facts about historical events and important people. When asked to interpret proverbs or figures of speech, though, Janine was in a quandary. "Why would I want to hit somebody with a hot iron?" she asked, when told to "strike while the iron is hot." Her literal interpretation also interfered with her understanding of the novels that she so dearly loved. She frequently missed the point of human interactions in the books or made mistaken assumptions about the motives of different characters. For Janine, it was important to provide direct instruction about figures of speech and multiple meanings. Her English teacher helped Janine make a glossary of the "expressions" in novels and plays. Her speech/language pathologist taught her clues that might identify something as abstract language. Armed with these strategies, Janine became more efficient in interpreting figures of speech and other abstract language. She also began to enjoy her reading more!

Literal interpretation and problems in central coherence also occur because the individual with AS may not automatically "step back" and consider the big picture. Joe was working on his comprehension questions for a book about Helen of Troy. He had answered many factual questions easily and accurately. Then he encountered, "What traits do Helen and Cassandra have in common?" He looked and looked for the answer. There was no place in the book that said, "Helen and Cassandra had the following traits in common . . . " Joe was stumped. After helping him understand the meaning of "trait," Joe's mother asked him to make a list of words or phrases that described Helen. Then he made a similar list for Cassandra. Joe's mom then asked him to look at both lists and see which traits were listed on both. With a "reframed" question, Joe was able to provide an accurate answer.

We must also recognize that a literal or detail-oriented approach is the most efficient way to solve some problems. Where would we be if there weren't software engineers to comb through lines of code to find the errors in computer programs? How would you understand this book if I didn't have a copy editor to find all the misspellings and grammatical errors? In science and mathematics, careful examination of details and their relationships to each other not only allows us to pinpoint errors but also to see patterns that may lead to new discoveries.

The critical point about AS and literal thinking, then, is to remember that literal thinking itself is neither good nor bad. Instead, we have to make sure that literal or detail-based thinking is one of several tools in our adolescents' cognitive tool kit. We have to make sure they can think in a literal or detail-based way when that's efficient and think in a more abstract or "big picture" manner when that's more appropriate.

SO, HOW CAN WE HELP?

As with any other aspect of helping our kids, our approach to literal thinking and problems in central coherence rests on understanding where, when, and why the adolescent doesn't get it. Then we can fashion opportunities for direct teaching of "how" to solve problems and think abstractly.

○ Just as we talked above about introducing new information through the adolescent's passions and preoccupations, we need to begin teaching about abstract thought by starting at the literal level that the adolescent uses so automatically. Think about the approach of Joe's mother. She knew that Joe was great at making lists of facts. She also knew that the novel included a great deal of factual information about the two characters. After Joe completed the literal task of listing character traits, he was able to use his strong analytical abilities to identify those that both characters had in common. In other words, Joe's mom translated an abstract, big picture task into a detail-oriented question.

○ We can use this detail-based approach for an amazing number of "abstract" questions. Venn diagrams, plot lines, and concept maps are concrete ways of approaching questions like "How were King David and King Solomon alike and different?" or "What events led to the development of written language?" or even "What are the key components of civilization?" You can find examples of these tools in the Appendix.

○ Once we teach a strategy, it's important to teach the adolescent when and where to use it. Dr. Jane Holmes Bernstein (originator of the zigger zagger) again offers a helpful technique: "zoom in, zoom out." Using the metaphor of the zoom lens on a camera, we teach the student to zoom in on information that requires a detail-oriented approach and to zoom out when a big picture approach is more efficient. "Sally, we need to brainstorm about things to give Dad for his birthday. Let's zoom out and think about all the things he might like." Or, "Sally, you need to edit your rough draft for spelling and grammar. Is this a zoom-in or a zoom-out situation?" For some adolescents, it's helpful to look through a camera or video lens to see the difference in what you see when zooming in or out.

○ Zooming out is critical to knowing what something is about. Ask, "What is this about?" frequently. Talk about movies, TV shows, books, and family gatherings. When the adolescent launches into a report of the movie or experience from start to finish, remind him or her to zoom back out. By the way, another way to ask "about" questions is, "If you had to give this a title, what would you call it?"

○ Just as a student learns to see the big picture, it's helpful to teach him or her how the parts of the whole relate to each other. For example, *Star Wars* is about "good and evil" and a young man's search for his identity. It also has a lot of odd-looking characters and spaceships rocketing around. Why did the moviemakers need to include all of this? Help your adolescent see the connections between and among ideas, facts, people, and the like.

○ Besides teaching when to use a detail-oriented vs. big picture approach, it's helpful to teach when to use other types of problem-solving strategies. Some adolescents benefit from compiling a notebook of task cards, flow charts, or algorithms to use in different problem-solving situations. When presented with a new problem, they can decide (with varying levels of assistance) which strategy fits the problem. For example, we might ask the adolescent to read a math word problem and then tell us which mathematical algorithm is most appropriate.

○ Once students with AS learn a strategy for solving a problem, they often tend to continue it. Sometimes that's fine. At other times, they pursue that approach past its usefulness. As a second-grader, Joe learned that he needed to mark out the original numeral and write in the new numeral when "borrowing" in subtraction. As a seventh grader, Joe's long division problems are so cluttered with slashed-out and rewritten numerals that even he can't read them. Joe doesn't need the slashes and new numerals for computation anymore, but he thinks this is what the teacher means when she says, "Show your work." When Joe's teacher assured him that he didn't need to use this method anymore, his accuracy and speed improved dramatically.

○ Just as students may need to be told when they don't need to use an outdated strategy anymore, they often benefit from the reminder to shift back and forth between strategies or interpretations. This is particularly true when they get stuck on one interpretation. Jane was writing a lab report for an experiment in which she added 3 milliliters of water to her solution every 2 minutes for 1/2 hour. In answering the question of how many milliliters of water she added altogether, Jane added 3+3+3+3+3+3+3+3+3+3+3+ 3+3+3+3. Asked why she did it this way, Jane replied that

"'Altogether' means addition, so I used addition." Her father helped her think of another way of solving the problem besides the cumbersome task of addition. "Oh, 'altogether' doesn't always mean add! I could also multiply!" Jane learned.

SHOWING WHAT YOU KNOW

As we all know, many adolescents with AS know a great deal. Showing that knowledge, especially on demand, is often another story. Problems in showing knowledge or skill on demand can arise from a number of sources. Adolescents may not understand exactly what we're asking them to show. One fifth grader thought that the reminder to use her "best handwriting" meant to add curlicues and flourishes! They may understand what we're asking, but remain unable to retrieve relevant information "on the spot." They may want to answer, but be unable to shift away from whatever is pre-occupying them at the moment. Or they may have trouble deciding what to say or write and what to leave out. After reading previous chapters, you'll recognize some of these inefficiencies as the results of the regulatory, communicative, or executive function glitches that can occur in AS. For the purposes of this chapter, it's helpful to consider what happens when an adolescent with AS tries to show what she knows in the cognitive domain.

Suzanne is a high school junior taking United States history. Her class just finished the unit on World War II. The take-home test included this question: "What influences made the U.S. slow to enter World War II? What factors caused the U.S. to enter the war?" Suzanne is a history buff. She knows about Franklin D. and Eleanor Roosevelt, Winston Churchill, and Joseph P. Kennedy. She read *No Ordinary Time*, Doris Kearns Goodwin's biography of the Roosevelts during the war years. She also knows that her answer can only be two pages long. Her paper began, "Franklin D. Roosevelt had polio when he was in his 20s. He was only able to walk a little bit after that. Newspaper photographers were not allowed to take pictures of him in his wheelchair . . . ." By the time Suzanne got to the war, she had written five pages. She also had used up precious time that she needed for other test questions. Even though she knew that her answer was only supposed to be two pages long, Suzanne didn't know what to leave out. Since she ran out of time, she decided to turn in what she had finished. After reading Suzanne's essay, her teacher wrote, "This is very interesting, Suzanne, but you didn't answer the questions. You could have made a bulleted list of factors for each question. You didn't need to tell me about polio, FDR's home in New York, or Joseph Kennedy's children."

Fortunately, Suzanne's history teacher also understood AS. He had a conference with Suzanne to talk about the country's entry into the war. As she talked, he jotted down critical points. He then gave her his notes and asked her to go back and write an essay about just those points. With the teacher's assistance in "scaffolding" her knowledge, Suzanne was able to write an A+ essay.

Suzanne is not alone in struggling to demonstrate her full range of knowledge through her written work. In fact, for many bright adolescents with AS, the only "educational handicap" that proves their need for special educational services is the discrepancy between what they know and what they can show in writing. When we consider the implicit tasks of writing (such as establishing your audience and knowing what to leave out as well as what to put in), it isn't surprising that written expression can be the bane of the existence of adolescents with AS.

SO, HOW CAN WE HELP?

The broken record again . . . we can't expect adolescents with AS to show what they know unless they are set from sensory, regulatory, and communicative standpoints. All of the strategies below are based upon the assumption that we've helped the adolescent become "available" for learning. That said, efficient demonstration of knowledge and skill often relies upon establishing automatic ways of organizing what you know.

○ Expressing what you know depends in part upon how the information was organized to begin with. The Venn diagrams, cause/effect maps, and the like, mentioned in the previous section, are useful ways of helping the student understand and organize information at the level of input.

○ The same tools can be used to organize output as well. For example, if Suzanne has a cause/effect diagram of our entry into WWII, she can use the content of each "cause" box as a bulleted item on her take-home answer. Or if Joe has a Venn diagram of the similarities and differences between Helen of Troy and Cassandra, he can use it to organize his "compare/contrast" paragraph.

○ Templates or algorithms for responding can be extremely helpful for adolescents with AS. Templates and algorithms are like formulas—once the student identifies which to use for a given question or assignment, he or she simply has to proceed through a series of over-learned steps. We can teach templates for decoding tricky words, for answering multiple-choice questions, and for multistep math problems. A sample algorithm is provided in the Appendix.

○ Templates are also remarkably useful for writing paragraphs, essays, and term papers. Each student (with or without AS) should have burned into his or her brain a format for writing a paragraph (topic sentence, supporting details, clincher sentence). (See page the Appendix for an example of a paragraph template.) These templates can then be customized for different types of paragraphs (for example, a descriptive paragraph versus a compare and contrast paragraph). Initially, it is helpful to have the student fill out a template form before writing the paragraph itself. As the template becomes second nature, the student may be able to refer mentally to the template while writing. For the student with AS, the template becomes most helpful in maintaining the coherence of the paragraph. He or she can be taught to question, "Is that detail related to my topic sentence?" As the student progresses to the essay level, he or she can ask, "Are all of these paragraphs related to my introductory paragraph?" or "Did I write about all of the things I mentioned in the intro?"

(More information is available from resources such as the *LINKS* curriculum or *Inspiration* software, listed in the Resources section at the end of the book.)

A FEW WORDS ABOUT NLD/RHD

Many parents of adolescents with AS have read Sue Thompson's book *The Source for Nonverbal Learning Disorders*. It's not hard to notice the similarities between nonverbal learning disorder (NLD) and AS. (Some professionals prefer the term "right hemisphere dysfunction/disorder" (RHD) to the NLD label.) No one knows the exact numbers, but it is generally accepted that a fairly large number of individuals with AS also fit the NLD/RHD profile.

What does this mean for thinking and learning? For adolescents with AS and characteristics of NLD/RHD, it means that we often see them struggle with mathematics and the sciences that rely upon mathematical computation or understanding. We tend to see inefficiencies in making sense of information presented in a visuospatial manner. Geometry, physics, and art can be overwhelming. Even familiar information can get lost in a sea of too much visual input. Finding something in a locker or cluttered room, making it to the right classroom at the beginning of the semester, and scanning a page for a critical word are examples of so-called "easy" tasks that can be frustratingly difficult. On a practical level, these students do better with written directions to a friend's house than they do with a map. They do better with memorizing lists of facts, definitions, or concepts than with imagery as a mnemonic strategy.

SO, HOW CAN WE HELP?

○ When developing worksheets, study guides, graphic organizers, or tests for students with AS and an NLD/RHD profile, be sensitive to the amount, arrangement, and type of information on a page. Leave plenty of room between items. Make clear distinctions between different types of information or problems. If the purpose of the task is to teach the student to shift back and forth between different types of problems (as with a math paper), emphasize in the directions that the student must read each problem carefully before starting to work.

○ When using a visual aid to explain and reinforce a concept, use words first. For example, you might say, "This chart is designed to help you understand the causes and effects of the Boston Tea Party. Each cause is written in a diamond shape. Each effect is written inside an oval. If an event started as the effect of one event, but then caused something else, you'll see a diamond with an oval around it . . . ." Then, in explaining more, "Let's think about the passage of the Stamp Tax by the English Parliament. Was that a cause or effect of the Tea Party? Right, that was a cause. We'll write that in this diamond here."

○ Teach mathematical operations through a list of steps. Task cards can be very helpful here, as they present a list of steps in sequential order.

○ Remain sensitive to any difficulty the student has with handwriting. Provide notes for lectures. Offer to take dictation when the student is required to fill in blanks on charts, and the like. If there is a discrepancy between what the student writes and what you think he/she knows, offer a conference to talk about the material.

A FINAL WORD

For many adolescents with AS, the cognitive arena offers a place to shine. Our task as adults is to work together to help the students get out of their own way, to help them show knowledge and skills efficiently, and to help them develop a repertoire of skills for adaptive and flexible thinking and learning. As we teach them "how," we're likely to be amazed by the breadth and depth of their understanding. And, if we listen closely, we'll often learn that their unique take on the world can lead us to perspectives that we never thought of before. The lessons we learn from them can become "peaks" in our journey through life.

CHAPTER SIX

Passions, Preoccupations, and Routines

As a young child, David was fascinated by trains. He particularly loved "Thomas the Tank Engine" and his fellow engines. David could recite all of the "Thomas" books and videos. When he played with his own trains, he re-enacted the stories exactly.

David's parents appreciated his interest in trains, but worried that "Thomas" might be considered too young for a preadolescent. When David was eight, his parents purchased an electric train set and built a layout in their basement.

Now, as an adolescent, David remains fascinated with trains. He enjoys running his trains around a layout that has become more and more elaborate. David spends every free moment reading train magazines. He attends every train show within 100 miles of his home. He has in-depth conversations with model railroad buffs two or three times his age. They are impressed with David's memory for detail, with the exactness of his scale models, and with his appreciation of the history of model railroading. The railroaders in his town and the surrounding area have become David's pals.

David's interest in trains is an example of the passions that can preoccupy the minds of individuals with Asperger Syndrome. In

David's case, he and his parents were able to use his childhood pre-occupation as the foundation for a hobby that provided social and intellectual satisfaction. Some families and adolescents are not able to achieve this transformation as easily, however. In this chapter, we'll talk about passions, preoccupations, and routines—how to understand them, when (and when not) to tolerate them, and how they can sometimes be used to the adolescent's advantage.

> Many of the passions, preoccupations, and routines described in this chapter could fall under headings such as "rituals" or "obsessions." While certain patterns of thought and behavior in people with AS do indeed meet the definition of rituals or obsessions, this chapter uses the terms "passions," "preoccupations," and "routines." This is done intentionally—to remind all of us that not every all-encompassing interest or repetitive behavior is pathological. ✺

BUT, BEFORE WE START, REMEMBER: YOU CAN LEAD A HORSE TO WATER . . .

When our children are younger, we can introduce interventions and modifications in a relatively one-sided manner. We decide what they need to change, rearrange the environment in order to help them change, and provide consequences for their efforts (or lack thereof).

This seldom works with adolescents, however. Even though adolescents with AS may not seem as mature emotionally as their typically developing peers, they usually do have strong feelings about independence and personal choice. No matter how objectionable we may find an interest or behavior, we're unlikely to change it substantially without the "buy-in" of the adolescent.

While this "buy-in" is important in any intervention or modification we attempt with adolescents, it's particularly important in the area of passions and preoccupations. (Just think about how you'd feel if someone announced to you that you had to give up your favorite pastime just because someone else thought it was "inappropriate.") As we consider passions, preoccupations, and routines, we must constantly remind ourselves that our efforts will be most successful if undertaken within the context of a working partnership with our adolescent.

THE NATURE OF PASSION, PREOCCUPATION, AND ROUTINE

Most of us have interests or hobbies that fascinate us, soothe ruffled feelings, or prevent boredom. For adolescents with AS, though, interests and hobbies can take on a different level of intensity. In AS, passions, preoccupations, and routines can be akin to rituals. In a way, they are the mental equivalent of the repetitive behaviors seen in many children with other types of autism spectrum disorders. In other ways, they are similar to the characteristic symptoms of obsessive compulsive behavior. Regardless of their labels, passions, preoccupations, and routines can be soothing or disturbing, transient or long-lasting.

One of the questions that most parents ask is, "When should I tolerate it, and when should I intervene?" Unfortunately, there is no single answer to this question. But there are a few questions to consider:

○ Does the passion, preoccupation, or routine serve a functional purpose, such as reducing anxiety, relieving boredom, or soothing frustration?

○ Might the passion, preoccupation, or routine lead eventually to a broader range of interests or skills, especially in the social realm?

○ Does the passion, preoccupation, or routine prevent the adolescent from participating in the usual and adaptive aspects of everyday life?

○ Does the passion, preoccupation, or routine disturb others or violate developmentally appropriate standards of behavior?

○ Does the passion, preoccupation, or routine cause harm (physical or emotional) to anyone?

In general, if the passion, preoccupation, or routine does not cause immediate harm, our best strategy is to use the adolescent's interest to build toward something more adaptive and developmentally "mainstream." We'll talk about specific ways to do this in the sections below.

One other common question (often from adolescents with AS) is, "What's wrong with being interested in just one thing? Maybe I'm just going to grow up to be Albert Einstein or Thomas A. Edison." This question does have at least one answer: "We never want to take away a passion, preoccupation, or routine that is safe. But we do want to make sure that you have a range of skills. We want you to grow up to have choices, not to be stuck in a rut because we didn't help you check out other options."

PASSIONS, PREOCCUPATIONS, ROUTINES, AND THE REGULATION OF INPUT AND ALERTNESS

Some passions, preoccupations, and routines arise from the individual's need to control sensory information or to provide input that is calming or alerting. These needs may result in behaviors that seem repetitive or ritualistic. Rubbing a spot on the arm, chewing the inside of the cheek, hand wringing, tapping, or repetitive touching are examples of actions that probably began as a self-regulatory attempt. Over time, these can become habits. The adolescent often is unaware that he or she is doing whatever it is. If asked to stop doing whatever it is, the adolescent is likely to develop another behavior that serves the same regulatory purpose.

A seventh grader named Rocky leaned his chair back constantly. When told that he had to keep six feet on the floor at all times (his two and the chair's four), he began to rock back and forth in his chair. From the standpoint of Rocky's teacher and classmates, the rhythmic rocking was even more disruptive than leaning the chair back. The teacher rued the day she told him to keep six feet on the floor.

The occupational therapist explained that chair leaning and rocking served the same purpose—helping Rocky pay attention by providing input into his vestibular system. But tilting the chair was unsafe, and rocking was disruptive. The occupational therapist worked with Rocky and his teacher to devise some neck and shoulder rolls that gave him similar sensory input. The teacher then instructed all of the students to do their "exercises" at the beginning of class to "wake up their brains."

Most of us have our favorite repetitive behaviors. We use them to reduce anxiety, to relieve boredom, or to perk ourselves up. Watch others around you at a meeting or even at a party. People doodle, tap their pencils, chew on their pens, tear Styrofoam cups into pieces, rub their foreheads, twirl their hair, or stroke their beards. Think about what you do to stay alert or to settle yourself down. Sitting down for a cup of tea, glancing through the newspaper before leaving the house, humming a tune, or playing a game of computer solitaire before starting to work are all socially accepted rituals.

For folks without AS, it's reasonably easy to discern what behavior is acceptable within a given situation. We also recognize that repetitive behaviors that were once condoned may no longer be looked upon kindly (witness cigarette smoking). Once we determine what's appropriate to the context, we find ways of meeting our regulatory needs without looking too peculiar. Or if we can't get rid of the behavior entirely, we find ways of restricting it to private places (again, witness smoking).

One drawback of certain passions, preoccupations, and routines of adolescents with AS, though, is that they can disturb others or call negative attention to the individual. To be frank, some of the most satisfying self-regulatory behaviors of all should never be performed in the company of others. (If you don't know what these actions are, watch adolescent boys when they think no one is looking!) Yet adolescents with AS may continue to use these strategies to self-regulate even after their peers have learned greater discretion. The adolescent with AS is more prone to violate social norms for self-regulatory behavior for several reasons: He or she may not realize that other people get "grossed out" by their behavior; he or she may not be aware of the action or its purpose; or he or she may not have developed other age-appropriate regulatory strategies.

SO, HOW CAN WE HELP?

Before deciding to "help," return to the questions listed on page 95. It's important to make an active choice about whether the passion, preoccupation, or routine is something that may need to be changed. If you and the adolescent do decide to change things, the following suggestions may prove successful.

CLEAR AND DIRECT FEEDBACK

The first rule of thumb here is to provide clear and direct feedback for the adolescent with AS. "Clear and direct" need not mean "critical." Instead, we need to remember that the adolescent with AS is likely to have a social knowledge deficit that keeps him or her from realizing the impact of the action.

As a younger child, Rosannah Young frequently sat with her hands tucked under her arms or under her legs. Rosannah said that this felt good, because it made her feel that she was "all in one piece." Prior to puberty, no one thought much of this. As her body developed, however, her parents and teachers became slightly more concerned about the possible sexual implications.

"Remember how we talked about tucking in your hands?" Rosannah's mother opened.

"Yeah. Sometimes I don't know what to do with my hands. This keeps them from flying away," Rosannah replied.

"That worked when you were younger, Rosannah. And I understand why it works for you. But now that you're growing into a young woman, other people may not understand it the same way," continued Mrs. Young.

"What will they think?" questioned Rosannah.

"They may think you're touching your breasts or genital area on purpose," Mrs. Young resolutely responded.

"Oh, that is disgusting!! Why do people have such dirty minds?" replied a shocked Rosannah.

"It's not really disgusting, Rosannah. It's just what some people think. I wanted you to know that that's what some people, especially kids your age, might think."

This step of providing clear and direct feedback can often be quite frustrating for parents and teachers. This is because we may be faced with trying to explain things that aren't totally logical. If Rosannah had no sexual intent, why should others interpret her behavior in those terms? If it's okay to scratch your back in public, why isn't it okay to scratch your bottom? (And if you're tired, why can't you rest your elbows on the dinner table?)

When all else fails in helping the adolescent with AS understand the impact of self-regulatory behavior, try this: "You're right. This doesn't make logical sense. But lots of folks (kids/adults/teachers) feel this way. I just wanted you to know what other people might think when you do that."

THE PURPOSE OF THE BEHAVIOR

As we said above, it's important to identify the purpose served by the adolescent's self-regulatory behavior. This can be quite difficult at times, because there may actually be several purposes. Or the original purpose may have been quite different from the current one. In addition, many adolescents with AS aren't particularly good observers of their own minds or bodies. If this is the case, they literally may not know why they do what they do.

We can try something like the following exchange between Rosannah and Mrs. Young:

"Rosannah, I always wondered what you meant when you said that your hands might fly away if you don't tuck them in," Mrs. Young began.

"Well, Mom, don't you have trouble remembering where to put your hands so they don't fly away?"

"No, I've never had trouble with that. It sounds like you need some extra sensory info to help you with your hands, though. Let's

brainstorm about what you could do instead of tucking them in,"
Mrs. Young suggested.

"Hey, do we have any of those stress balls? Maybe I could
squeeze one of those when I'm just sitting and listening."

What they realized was that Rosannah did have trouble with a
sense of where her body was in space and that she also needed
"proprioceptive" and "tactile" input to help her pay attention.
Making an alliance to solve the problem allowed Rosannah to
brainstorm with her mom without feeling defensive. It also freed
Mrs. Young from that vicious cycle of threatening ("if you don't
stop that, I'll . . . "). Even if the stress balls don't work, Mrs. Young
has opened up a working partnership with Rosannah. This partnership will make it more likely that Rosannah and her mother will
eventually discover a strategy that serves the purpose and fits the
social and developmental context.

DEVELOPING ADAPTIVE BEHAVIORS

As our children grow older, it's important to think about lifelong
skills—for self-regulation, stress management, and leisure time.
These skills may involve pursuit of hobbies or passions. Drawing,
writing, reading, collecting, and building are pursuits that relieve
stress and bring satisfaction. The passions and preoccupations of
adolescents with AS can often be built into these "prosocial" stress
relievers. An obsession about who is on what coin can lead to a
hobby of coin collecting. Fascination with small appliances can
lead to a home fix-it shop. Preoccupation with computer hardware
can lead to consultation with classroom teachers over their balky
machines. Transforming passions into "adaptive alternatives" provides avenues for social and emotional growth.

One of the most neglected avenues for many of today's children
and adolescents is that of physical activity and regular exercise.
Unfortunately, many individuals with AS feel so clumsy and
unrewarded by physical activity that they avoid the most efficient
stress management and self-regulatory strategies of all. By adolescence, they've experienced the frustration of striking out at Little
League, kicking the ball in the wrong soccer goal, and mastering a

two-wheeler long after their peers (if at all). Their constraints in
"social sense" often extend to constraints in on the court or on the
field in team sports. It's no wonder that by adolescence, most individuals with AS would sooner avoid than participate in sports.

As the adults, it is extremely important for us to help adolescents with AS develop an exercise or fitness program that matches
their skills and interests. Many are more comfortable with sports
that don't involve balls. Swimming is an excellent alternative for
many with AS, as the water pressure gives input regarding the
position of one's body in space. (For some adolescents with AS,
swimming classes can be quite frustrating because of limited
attention and/or coordination—consider private lessons or ther-
apeutic swimming.) Running, biking, and weightlifting (with
appropriate instruction) are other pastimes that may be less challenging for the adolescent with coordination difficulties. For
adolescents in the right circumstances (geographically and finan-
cially), skiing, snowboarding, and inline skating can be reward-
ing. The goals of physical activity are primarily twofold: to
achieve reasonable levels of fitness and to provide a physical out-
let for stress. If we're lucky, the adolescent also achieves the
added benefit of developing an interest that connects him or her
with others.

Another oft-neglected regulatory mechanism is playing and/or
listening to music. Some children and adolescents with AS shy away
from music lessons because their visuospatial difficulties make it
challenging to read music. But for most individuals with AS, learning an instrument brings enormous payoffs. Learning to read music
and to understand its patterns seems to help many children (with
or without AS) with pattern recognition and mathematics.
Coordinating hands, eyes, and sometimes the mouth to produce
musical notes becomes an unexpected "occupational therapy." Some
parents swear that their offspring chewed less on shirt collars and
the like after taking up an instrument that requires blowing. Listening to music can be soothing and learning all the lyrics, musicians,
and composers fits nicely with the AS preoccupation with lists.
Finally, participation in music often helps the adolescent come in
contact with other people around shared passions. Think back to
your high-school days: Weren't the music/art/drama kids usually the
most accepting of individual differences?

PASSIONS, PREOCCUPATIONS, ROUTINES, AND PREDICTABILITY

Some passions, preoccupations, and routines develop out of the adolescent's need for predictability. Some of the classic AS preoccupations (such as train schedules and TV listings) highlight this need quite clearly.

Why do our adolescents need predictability? Without some degree of predictability, all of us feel anxious. The more unpredictable, the more chaotic the world feels. The more chaotic, the more anxious we feel. Even in adolescence, the world can seem a pretty chaotic place to someone with AS. The value of preoccupations and routines is that they introduce some predictability and control into an environment that seems otherwise confusing and capricious. In so doing, routines can reduce anxiety.

Seventeen-year-old Alice ate the same breakfast every morning. She kept her own personal box of Total (labeled with her name) on the middle shelf of the pantry. She used the same bowl, the same spoon, and the same glass every morning. She counted out the raisins as she added them to her bowl, then measured out 1/4 cup of 1% milk. When her younger brother decided to get her goat by moving the cereal or drinking all the 1% milk, Alice "freaked." Why, Alice's parents asked, did she have to be so selfish and controlling?

Alice rode a crowded bus to a large public high school every day. Because the bus route was so long, she never knew exactly when the bus would arrive at her stop. She also didn't know whether she'd be able to get a seat near the front. Alice couldn't stand the noise at the back of the bus. Once she got to school, Alice had to work hard to find her classes. Even halfway into the school year, she was easily confused by the visual and auditory overload in the hallways. By the time she arrived at her first period class, Alice felt overwhelmed by confusion. If all had gone well at breakfast, though, she could remember that orderliness and settle herself down.

For Alice and others, passions, preoccupations, and routines allow them to reduce their confusion and anxiety by carving out one little piece of life where everything goes according to plan. Alice isn't being controlling in the selfish sense of the word. She's simply trying to control her environment enough so that she can make it through the day.

It's not just the sensory overload that leads to increased need for predictability; it's also the social-communicative load. Few of us are predictable communicators. Our response may be determined by a whole host of factors that may or may not be related to our communicative partner (including whether or not someone ate our favorite breakfast food!). But for adolescents with AS, our communicative unpredictability can be devastating. As Alice asked, "How can she be so friendly on the phone and then walk right past me in the hall at school?" Or "Why does my mother get onto my brother when he hides my cereal but not say a word when he drinks all the milk?"

One attraction of most routines is that they involve inanimate objects. Objects don't have feelings. They stay where you put them. You don't have to consider their needs. Object-based routines can be very soothing, as they can truly be unchanging and repetitive.

SO, HOW CAN WE HELP?

The biggest challenge in changing the routines of an adolescent with AS is that he or she usually does not want to change. Thus, we really need to consider the five questions listed earlier in the chapter before we venture forth on a mission that is likely to create some conflict. And we are likely to ask ourselves repeatedly, "Why am I doing this?" In general, there are three reasons that we decide to interrupt the preoccupations and routines of an adolescent with AS: the routine is beginning to interfere with the adolescent's everyday life; the routine is beginning to interfere with the everyday life of those around him or her; or the routine is reinforcing the adolescent's tendency to be inflexible in the first place.

Once we decide that the routine must be addressed, it's important to return again to strategies described in other parts of this book. We must establish or cement our working partnership with the adolescent, provide clear and direct feedback about the behavior that concerns us, and identify the purpose(s) of the passion, preoccupation, or routine. Don't forget to address the "magical thinking" that may be involved here. Often routines and rituals are accompanied by a belief such as "If I don't do _____, then _____ will happen." If magical thinking is involved, we'll have to be especially careful in setting up the intervention plan. In other words, we'll have to make sure that none of the magical thoughts can come true!

We then turn to consideration of what all of us would like to accomplish: ideally, a continued sense of predictability and security without undue restriction of the lives of anyone involved.

1. IDENTIFY A REASONABLE ENDPOINT OR GOAL

For Alice, a reasonable endpoint was that she could eat a different kind of cereal or drink a different "level" of milk if she found "her kind" missing. For another adolescent who had tantrums whenever anyone moved his stuff, a reasonable endpoint might be to meet such glitches with an "Oh, well" and ten sequences of slow, deep breathing. Once the reasonable endpoint is identified and agreed upon, we can help the adolescent develop a series of small steps toward that endpoint.

2. DEVELOP A "HIERARCHY" OF STEPS TOWARD THE ENDPOINT OR GOAL

What is the smallest imaginable change in the current routine? (Maybe a different spoon for Alice's cereal?) Write that on a Post-it® note. Now move on to the next smallest change and so forth. Make sure that the first several steps are very easy to achieve. This sets up behavioral momentum and increases the adolescent's confidence.

Once you have a list of the steps toward the endpoint, review the list. Each step should be just a little harder than the step before it. If the steps don't proceed in order of increasing difficulty, rearrange the order (hence, the need for Post-its®!).

3. IDENTIFY STRATEGIES TO COPE WITH ANY DISCOMFORT THAT ACCOMPANIES THE CHANGES

Some adolescents respond well to relaxation strategies such as controlled breathing, progressive muscle relaxation, or imagery. Some find comfort in self-affirming statements ("I can do this. I know I can do this."). Others do well by repeating favorite lines from movies, books, or poems or singing a favorite song. Others find certain sensory inputs calming. Once you identify what works to calm the adolescent, have him or her use that strategy prior to any planned change in routine. Encourage the adolescent to repeat that strategy whenever he or she feels anxious.

4. IDENTIFY THE REINFORCERS FOR THE CHANGE

What will be the positive outcome of mastering each step? What will be the positive outcome for reaching and maintaining the endpoint?

While it would be wonderful for every adolescent to achieve his or her goal just for the sake of self-satisfaction, that probably isn't realistic. (Could I give up chocolate just because it's bad for me? No way!) When we're working with our adolescents on changing entrenched behaviors, we usually do need to provide an external reinforcement, but it needn't be extravagant. The most effective reinforcers are those that can be delivered naturally and (eventually) by the adolescent, and those that lead to the development or appreciation of something important. Sometimes, extra time to pursue a passion (not the one you're working on) is the best reward of all.

5. DECIDE WHAT OTHERS WILL KNOW ABOUT THE PROCESS

If this change process is happening at home, it will be important to talk with the adolescent about what he or she wants siblings or other family members to know. It's always best to tell them something, if only to ensure that they don't sabotage the whole process (intentionally or otherwise).

If the change process is happening at school or in the community, decide what adults and peers will be told. If the adolescent with AS has a buddy or favorite teacher, it's often helpful to bring him or her in on the plan (and often on the reinforcement).

If the adolescent with AS doesn't want anyone to know, abide by his or her wishes initially. If others unwittingly (or wittingly) interfere with the plan, you can have a problem-solving session to determine how to handle the behavior of others and whether to tell them more.

6. SET UP THE SCHEDULE AND BEGIN!

This is another important time for collaboration. How long does the adolescent think he or she needs to stay at one step before moving on to the next? How should you handle "lapses" (days when he or she just can't make the change)? Once you agree upon a schedule, write it on a calendar and post it in an agreed-upon place (again, bend to the adolescent's need for privacy).

Then begin! In the beginning, don't go to great lengths to avoid change or to create it. Just let the social environment function the way it typically does. If you live in a remarkably predictable household and no challenges arise, you may want to introduce very minor glitches into the routine. If you take this step, though, make sure that the glitches look natural, not contrived.

7. PROVIDE PRAISE FOR SUCCESS AND NONJUDGMENTAL PROBLEM SOLVING FOR LAPSES

It's likely that this change process will be tough, especially in the beginning. It's important for the adults to provide praise early and often, for even the smallest approximation to success. It's equally important not to take it personally when there are lapses. If given permission to share information about the change process with others in the home or school setting, ensure that they are equally positive and nonjudgmental.

Remember that a lapse is not a "relapse." A lapse is just a mistake or a bad day.

8. REVIEW PROGRESS AND PROVIDE CONGRATULATIONS AT THE MASTERY OF EACH STEP

As you praise the adolescent, don't forget to review how far he or she has come: "Wow, you thought that step would be really hard. And now you've done it." It's also helpful to think about what may have supported success. "What made it easier to change to a different cereal this week?"

9. MODEL FLEXIBILITY IN YOUR OWN ROUTINES

During the change process, pay special attention to your own routines (and, yes, we all have them!). Comment when you make a change and speculate out loud about its effect. When the adolescent is in the car with you, experiment with different routes to common destinations. Change the weekly menu! Wear a different color! Communicate that "flexibility is the spice of life"!

PASSIONS, PREOCCUPATIONS, ROUTINES, AND SATISFACTION

Larry was an adolescent in the rural Midwest. He wasn't much of a socializer. Some said he wasn't much of a student. But Larry had a passion and a routine. He shot 300 foul shots every day, even if the basketball team had a tough practice. If his mother made dinner before he finished his 300 shots, he went back outside in the dark to finish them.

Larry went to a major university and played varsity basketball. His team won many games. Larry kept on shooting 300 extra foul shots every day. He was the quintessential "gym rat." Larry went on to play in the professional ranks, for an East Coast basketball dynasty that wore green and white uniforms. Larry and his teammates won many championships and played in some of the classic contests of the 1980s. He kept shooting 300 extra foul shots every day. He remained a gym rat. When injuries forced him to retire, he went on to coach another pro team and to lead them to the finals of the playoffs. Larry imparted fundamentals (such as foul shooting) to his players.

Larry Bird doesn't have AS. He did have an all-encompassing passion and a routine to go along with that passion.

Some passions, preoccupations, and routines don't interfere with anyone. They don't cause harm. They don't restrict the adolescent from learning new skills or exploring new interests. They bring satisfaction, confidence, and sometimes a life's work. We don't need to worry about changing these.

PASSIONS, PREOCCUPATIONS, ROUTINES, OBSESSIONS, AND COMPULSIONS

Most of the passions, preoccupations, and routines described in this chapter are relatively safe. Most of them are pursued without causing great anxiety or distress for the adolescent. Thus, we seek to change these only when they interfere with daily functioning or disturb others.

Unfortunately, passions, preoccupations, and routines can sometimes be more problematic. They can cause physical or emotional harm. Or their pursuit can interfere with current or future functioning. Or they can appear as obsessions (repetitive thoughts) or compulsions (repetitive behaviors).

Terms such as "obsessive compulsive" have come to mean many things in our everyday vocabulary. Sometimes, we use the term to refer to a precise, meticulous, and predictable person. In mental health vocabulary, however, obsessions and compulsions are serious challenges, that interfere substantially with the person's everyday life (and often with the lives of those around him or her). They are also thought to cause distress to the individual. But the jury is still out on whether the repetitive thoughts and actions of individuals with AS are truly obsessions and compulsions. This is because most people with AS find comfort rather than distress in many of their repetitive thoughts and actions.

If the adolescent's passions, preoccupations, or routines cause harm, interfere with daily life, or create great distress, it is absolutely necessary to seek professional help. Combinations of individualized cognitive behavioral therapy, family interventions, and some medications have been found quite effective for adolescents with these challenges.

A FINAL NOTE

Passions, preoccupations, and routines vary from one adolescent with AS to another. Some are long-lasting and all-encompassing. Others are intense and brief. Some interfere with life or disturb other people. A few are truly harmful.

By creating a working partnership with our adolescents and by analyzing the advantages and drawbacks of passions, preoccupations, and routines, we can move everyone toward a more adaptive and flexible way of living.

Don't forget—"love makes the world go 'round." Since it's true, let's use it to help our adolescents expand their horizons.

CHAPTER SEVEN

Emotional Competence

Overheard in the middle school halls:

"Just because I think she's cute doesn't mean I want to go out with her."

"I thought I was gonna die. She said, 'Get lost, loser' in front of the whole cafeteria."

"I feel concerned every day. I'm always worried about something."

"I need to sleep til 11 tomorrow. I'm wasted."

"I can't believe they gave us two tests on the same day that two projects are due. I'm really ticked off."

"Do you believe my mother wants to stay at the mall with us? In every single store?"

"Why don't you come over and we'll eat junk food and watch videos?"

"AWE-SOME!!!"

Emotional competence refers to our ability to recognize and identify our feelings, to understand them, to express them in an adaptive way, and to cope. It allows us to link emotions with experiences—"I'm frustrated because I can't find my homework." It allows us to voice those connections to ourselves or to others—

"I can't believe I lost my paper again! ARGGHH!" It allows coping and modulation and, sometimes, requests for help—"Darn! Can you help find my paper?" or "Mrs. Jones, I did my math. I just can't find it in my house. Can I turn it in tomorrow?" With reasonable levels of emotional competence, a person can feel feelings and still operate within the behavioral norms of his or her community.

Emotional competence is a journey, not a destination. Just when we think we've arrived, life throws us another curve. Many children achieve reasonable levels of emotional competence, just in time for adolescence to throw them that curve! For adolescents with Asperger Syndrome, though, the emotional tasks of childhood may not have been completed before puberty begins. Whether they can admit it or not, they often need our help in achieving a level of emotional competence that supports everyday functioning at home, in school, and in the community.

Most adults feel relatively confident of their ability to help young children with their feelings. It seems pretty easy to soothe feelings that were hurt by a teasing peer or a lost toy. Even the anger of a "little kid" feels manageable to most adults. And little kids are so appreciative of our attention and assistance.

But many of us quake in our boots when faced with the task of helping an adolescent with his or her feelings. Maybe those feelings feel so intense that we hesitate to meet them head on. Maybe our adolescent is expressing feelings that we aren't sure that we've mastered. Maybe our own adolescence is still too fresh in our minds. Maybe we don't know how to react to the "push-pull" of adolescent feelings, such as "Mom, stay out of my sight. I hate you. Can you take me and Jennifer to the mall?" And as parents and teachers of adolescents with AS, maybe we're overwhelmed with our fears about the implications of the feelings—"If he feels so angry, what will he do if there's no one there to talk him down?"

As with every other dilemma posed in this book, there's no single answer to the question of "What do I do about my child's emotions?" What we do know, however, is that we have to build on our working partnership with the adolescent and listen—with our ears, our eyes, our hearts, and our brains.

EMOTIONAL TASKS OF ADOLESCENTS

- ○ Knowing how you feel
- ○ Knowing why you feel the way you feel
- ○ Expressing how you feel to the "right" people in the "right" way
- ○ Coping with the feeling, so it doesn't take over your life and/or ruin your behavior
- ○ Forming an identity and value system

KNOWING HOW YOU FEEL—RECOGNIZING AND IDENTIFYING FEELINGS

Adolescence often brings with it a host of feelings that seem unfamiliar. Many of the basic feelings are the same, but they're mixed together in unexpected combinations. Affection for your best friend can coexist with jealousy over her ability to flirt with the boys. Admiration of your buddy can be mixed with intense competition in the classroom or on the field. Love for and dependence on your parents sit beside wishing that they didn't exist. It's not surprising that adolescents in general often get confused about which emotional end is up!

For the adolescent with AS, the task of recognizing and identifying feelings can be even more of a challenge. Many children with AS don't have a "mental map" of their bodies—they have trouble knowing where they are in space, organizing their physical response to the world, and recognizing where physical sensations come from. Over the years, I've noticed that the children with poor mental maps of their bodies also tend to have inaccurate mental maps of their minds. In other words, they may not know what they feel. Or if they do know that they're feeling something, they may not have the words to label it. Or they may have been so preoccupied with something else that they didn't notice their emotional reaction at the time.

Some adolescents with AS find feelings annoying. One's own feelings can't be seen, touched, or measured quantitatively. Thus, emotions can be difficult for adolescents with AS to think about, much less label. As one young man told me, "What's all this fuss about feelings?"

SO, HOW CAN WE HELP?

Remember that no one strategy works for everyone. In your working partnership with your child (or student), you'll learn what works best. These are some hints that have worked for others.

MODELING

It's easier to learn to recognize feelings if you live with or go to school with people who recognize and voice their own feelings. Modeling this awareness is an important first step in teaching adolescents with AS to identify their own feelings.

But, beware! Recognizing and identifying feelings doesn't necessarily mean expressing them intensely. In fact, a parent or teacher's frequent and intense expression of emotion can actually befuddle an adolescent with AS. He or she may not be able to make the connection between the emotional display and the causes for it. When modeling the identification of feelings, it's best if we talk about it rather than act it out. "Boy, I'm so mad!" "I feel really frustrated. I worked on that project all day and didn't get anything done." "I'm worried about Grandma. She doesn't seem to be getting over that cold of hers."

Some parents and teachers of adolescents with AS are hesitant to voice their feelings. They understandably fear that such emotional expression will overwhelm the adolescent. Certainly, some adolescents are overwhelmed by emotional expression. Most of the time, though, they are able to handle another person's identification of emotion, as long as the intensity is controlled. In fact, sometimes they are even fascinated and curious. One girl I know offered to intervene in her parents' marital dispute because she could be "cool headed" and they couldn't! (Her parents wisely declined the offer.)

LEARNING TO SELF-MONITOR

This strategy is built upon the assumption that the adolescent may not have a mental map of his or her mind. It begins with providing feedback about what the adolescent looks like when he or she feels a certain way. The adult might say something like, "You're all slumped over. You're hardly talking. I wonder if you're sad about something." Sometimes, I have families make observations and fill them in on a chart like the sample below:

FEELINGS CHART	
Physical Sign	**Emotion**
Moving fast, laughing	Happy or excited
Hunched shoulders	Tense or worried
Fast speech and clenched teeth	Irritated or annoyed
Lying around, not talking	Sad or down in the dumps
Red face, rising voice volume	Angry and getting angrier

As adolescents become more accustomed to feedback about the outward and physical signs of their feelings, they are likely to begin to use the labels on their own. Eventually, they begin to link internal states with emotions. "It feels like my brain is getting hot inside. I think I'm mad." "My insides are all shaky. I'm nervous."

AND WHEN THEY DO LABEL THE FEELINGS . . .

When we've waited "for years" for the adolescent to label his or her feelings, we're understandably excited when it finally happens. When it does happen, we can't rush in to "fix" the feeling or problem. This is when it's most important to listen, listen, listen—not to fix, preach, or downplay. Keep your focus on what the adolescent is saying. Help him or her describe more about the feeling. "A hot brain, huh? What's that like?" or "Are all of your insides shaky, or just some parts?" "What kind of mad—just a little irritated or very mad?"

Sometimes the adolescent identifies feelings that are upsetting or worrisome to us. This is probably most evident when they express angry or aggressive feelings or when they reveal sadness and desperation. Probably nothing in life truly prepares us for the experience of hearing these feelings, and our first reaction is to try to fix the feelings or to sweep them away. The angry feelings may be addressed toward us, in what sounds like disrespect. In these instances, it's even more important to listen and to try to understand precisely what the adolescent is saying. Once we understand exactly what the adolescent feels, we can move on to the problem-solving strategies described later in the chapter.

KNOWING WHY YOU FEEL THE WAY YOU FEEL— MAKING EMOTION/EVENT CONNECTIONS

Many adolescents with AS are able to identify their feelings. They just don't understand the reasons behind the emotions.

Fourteen-year-old Ken had been irritable for a while. Neither he nor his parents knew exactly why. They did know that he blew up over the slightest thing and that even a simple request (such as "Brush your teeth, please") could lead to tears.

Just before Christmas vacation, Ken suddenly began to protest going to school in the morning. He said he felt too tired. His parents also noticed that he was having trouble falling asleep at night, and they assumed that he probably was tired. They wondered, though, if there was something going on at school. Everyone assumed that Christmas break would give Ken a chance to catch up on sleep. They figured that he would return to school after the holidays bright-eyed and bushy-tailed.

Instead, Ken felt worse. He burst into tears at the thought of school. Neither his parents nor his school counselor could put their finger on the problem. Ken insisted that he was "just tired and upset." He didn't know why he was upset.

Ken finally was able to return to school once he was assured that he could come to the counselor's office whenever he felt overwhelmed. Knowing that he had this "out" allowed Ken to relax a little and to attend classes. Simultaneously, the family changed their evening routine to make sure that Ken and the rest of the family settled down earlier at night.

Still, no one knew exactly what was bothering Ken.

Like many adolescents with AS, Ken had trouble understanding his emotions because he was not a very good observer of his own mind. He didn't usually notice what was going on when a certain feeling arose. Even when he did notice, he didn't make connections between that event/feeling and prior similar experiences. As with many adolescents with AS, experiences were stored in his memory in separate "compartments," and it wasn't easy for him to make comparisons between the current situation and the past.

Understanding our emotions depends upon the capacity to make these connections. But adolescents with AS are often too overwhelmed with the sensory, cognitive, and social aspects of a situation to notice their inner state. The opportunity for making event/emotion connections may pass before the adolescent has the chance to "hook things together."

SO, HOW CAN WE HELP?

Sometimes we're lucky. We know the reasons for the adolescents' feelings and we can provide direct feedback about our ideas, at least as long as we can help them listen to us. At other times, we're as clueless as they are. Then we have to be detectives. As always, it's important to respect that the feelings are their feelings and not ours (even though their feelings do affect us). It's an especially important time to respect our working partnership with the adolescent.

WHEN WE HAVE A CLUE . . .

When we have a hunch about the reasons for the adolescent's emotions, our "only" challenge is in conveying our idea and testing its usefulness. Although it sounds simple, it usually requires all of the delicacy of brain surgery. Dogmatic presentations ("You're just feeling that way because . . . .") are doomed. Prescriptions are equally perilous ("You'll get over it if you . . . ."). Recalling one's own adolescence often turns off the adolescent's "listening ears" (remember when your parents talked about walking two miles to school in the snow?).

After listening (and listening and listening), we might try a remark such as "I wonder what's going on?" If the adolescent doesn't know, we might venture farther: "I might have a hunch. Do you want to hear it?" If the adolescent says "no," then don't offer your idea. As Shakespeare wrote, "Ripeness is all." None of us is ready to hear something until we're ready to hear it.

If the adolescent is ready to hear our ideas, we can present them as hypotheses. "This is just a guess, but I wonder if you're feeling that way because . . . ." "I might be missing the boat, but my reaction was . . . ." Be ready to back up your hypothesis with concrete evidence. Then ask if that theory makes any sense.

Some parents ask why they should be so tentative or act so befuddled when they "know" what is happening. There are several reasons: We want to emphasize that this is a partnership, not a dictatorship; we want the adolescent to consider the validity of our suggestions, not just accept them "whole hog"; and we want to demonstrate and reinforce that none of us has all the answers where emotions are concerned.

Other parents ask if they should follow this strategy when the situation is urgent and dangerous. My bias is that an urgent or dangerous situation often means skipping the "understanding" step—we want to know how the adolescent feels and we want to keep everyone safe. This usually isn't the time to speculate or explore. We also need to make sure that we have a team involved: parents, educators, and mental health professionals to address the urgency in a comprehensive way.

WHEN YOU DON'T HAVE A CLUE . . .

Unfortunately, it's common that no one has the immediate answer about why the adolescent feels the way he or she feels. We can usually figure it out by working together, though.

o   Get as clear a description of the feeling as possible. Include both the emotional and physical aspects of the feeling.
o   Brainstorm to identify the "load" that the adolescent might be carrying at the moment. Don't forget to include sensory, communicative, and cognitive components of the load. For some adolescents, it helps to write the ideas on a big piece of paper as you go along, as this supports their working memory.
o   Identify any changes or stressors. No change is too "trivial" to leave out in your first analysis. Remember that transition and unpredictability can derail many adolescents with AS.

○ Make hypotheses about the connections between the current feeling(s) and experiences past and present.

○ Look at the "evidence" to determine if any of the theories make sense.

○ If you're using a Feelings Chart like the sample on page 111, add a third column entitled "Reasons." Then enter the reason on the chart.

Throughout this process, it's important to respect the adolescent's pace and style of reasoning. Many adolescents with AS can't move from the specific to the general easily (see Chapter Five, "Thinking and Learning"). Adolescents of any ilk may hesitate to accept an adult's reasoning. Both of these factors can make the process seem endless and/or doomed. Take your time.

The goal is not the finished product; the goal is to teach the adolescent a process of emotional problem solving.

And one more caution—this kind of analysis can't be done in the heat of the moment. None of us analyzes very well when we're upset. Adolescents with AS are even less efficient in emotional problem solving during times of upset.

EXPRESSING THE FEELING TO THE "RIGHT" PEOPLE IN THE "RIGHT" WAY

We often tell our children, "Feelings are never right or wrong. But there are wrong ways to express them." Obviously, achieving this goal is one of those lifelong tasks. Some of us are better at it than others. Even the best of us have times when we can't manage to get it "right," but knowing how to express feelings to the right people in the right way can be even more of a challenge for individuals with AS. In fact, accomplishing this kind of expression requires the use of all of the skills that are elusive to them: understanding one's own mental state, understanding the "emotional display rules" of the situation, recognizing the boundaries around disclosing personal information, finding the right words, and managing one's level of intensity.

As the adults, we have to set reasonable goals for emotional expression. When our adolescents are just learning to label and understand emotions, we can't blame them for awkward expression. On the other hand, we have to provide clear guidelines for behavior, since many youngsters with AS establish routines very quickly. In other words, we don't want to create future problems.

Through all of this, remember that adolescents with AS have trouble understanding the old adage, "It's not what you say. It's the way you say it."

SO, HOW CAN WE HELP?

EXPLICIT GUIDELINES

Make sure that the adolescent has "bought in." Try things like, "I know that other people want to hear your feelings. But it's hard to understand exactly what you mean when you express it that way. Can we work on how to express feelings in a way that people can hear?"

- Provide rules or guidelines about ways to express certain types of feelings. Make a chart of these.
- Demonstrate what you mean by "polite voice" or "non-threatening body language." Also demonstrate what is *not* a desirable way to express emotion.
- Help the adolescent practice. Reinforce any approximation to the desired behavior.
- Decide what types of feelings can be shared with which people. Put this on a chart. (See the discussion in Chapter Three about using a concentric circle chart to identify what kinds of things can be shared with which people.)

DEBRIEFING

- After the adolescent attempts to express emotion in "real life," talk about what worked and what didn't. By the way, don't try to do this in the midst of the emotional expression. This is best left for a quiet moment.
- Reinforce the adolescent's efforts, even if the result wasn't perfect. "You know, you used to show your anger by yelling

and stomping and name-calling. This time, you talked about your feelings in a tone I could understand. That was great!"
○ Ask for the adolescent's own assessment of the process. Don't forget to ask which mode of expression feels better, and don't be surprised if he or she says that yelling and screaming feels better (at least in the early stages).

One final point—just because the adolescent expressed emotions more adaptively, you don't necessarily have to grant his or her wishes. That's another question for another time!

COPING WITH THE FEELINGS

Fifteen-year-old Rebecca had been fortunate in the friends department. Even though she had struggled with emotional and behavioral control over the years, her small group of friends had stood by her. They knew how to take her rages with a grain of salt. They knew how to perk her up when she was feeling low. They did all of this because they valued her zany sense of humor, her creativity, and her generosity.

In tenth grade, the other girls became more interested in boys. In fact, they were "boy crazy." Rebecca wasn't there yet. She was still into horses, Pokèmon, and music. Her understanding of "love" and "relationships" went only as far as the romantic trials and tribulations of her favorite rock star. The other girls started to leave Rebecca out of their sleepovers. They were friendly when she called and nice to her at school, but they never called her.

Rebecca was devastated. She had worked hard to learn to make connections between her emotions and her experiences, and she knew the reason for her devastated feelings. She felt abandoned by her friends. Her feelings were so intense that she felt like "dissing" them or harming herself. She thought about starving herself so they would admire her thinness and pay attention to her. She wondered if she should invite them over and tell them her feelings.

> Fortunately, she also told her mother and her therapist about these feelings. They worked on other ways that Rebecca could cope with her very normal feelings of loss.

Adolescents with AS have all of the same feelings that other adolescents do. But they often lack the coping mechanisms to manage the feelings and still keep their behavior within a reasonably acceptable range. Their coping may be inefficient because they haven't had enough experience in understanding and managing feelings. Or the difficulty may relate to their sensory challenges (remember what happens if "your underwear is too tight"!). Many adolescents with AS don't have the circle of friends or the communicative sophistication needed to use relationships as a basis for coping. Additionally, their restricted range of interests may have boxed them in, keeping them from developing the strategies that other adolescents use to blow off steam.

SO, HOW CAN WE HELP?

Many adolescents believe that they are managing just fine, thank you very much. So they "don't need" the help of their parents or teachers. Adolescents with AS may be no different than from peers in this regard (although some do actively solicit help with coping). Our response must validate these feelings, while pointing out the "real world" effects of inefficient coping—"I know that you want to handle this your way, but I'm worried because you haven't been able to go to school seven out of the last ten days." Our efforts at teaching coping will be much more successful if the adolescent agrees that this is something worth addressing. As we model ways to achieve a working partnership around learning better coping skills, we can model a process of seeking and accepting help in the future.

BUILDING ADAPTIVE COPING SKILLS

- o Use the five-step process for developing self-regulation, described in Chapter Two, to discover soothing sensory strategies. For some adolescents, deep breathing, progressive relaxation, and/or imagery strategies can be soothing and relaxing.

○ It's important to help adolescents avoid catastrophic thinking. Practice reframing the current (supposedly horrible) situation is less extreme terms. "EVERYBODY will know" is more realistically "Jane and Sally heard it."

○ Consider ways in which the adolescent's passions and preoccupations can be used for calming or for self-reinforcement. For example, Rebecca was passionate about her music. She found that certain songs made her feel good about herself and about life.

○ Help the adolescent consider coping strategies for the immediate situation and for the longer term. For example, deep breathing and humming (to oneself) can help manage immediate frustration long enough to get out of the situation at hand. A longer-term coping strategy might involve something creative—working on a Claymation film, reading adventure novels, or finding a new hobby.

○ Don't forget to present exercise as a coping strategy. One young woman I know swims laps whenever she feels overwhelmed emotionally. Not only is the physical activity calming, but it also leads to a sense of competence. She says, "If I can swim a mile, I can do anything!"

○ Help the adolescent learn to self-monitor and self-reinforce: "I'm furious. But if I keep my temper under control at school, I'll splurge on a Coke and chips this afternoon."

○ Model talking with others as a coping strategy. Encourage your adolescent to do the same, and reinforce his or her efforts even when they aren't sophisticated or articulate.

○ Don't punish feelings.

○ Reinforce the adolescent's efforts, no matter how awkward. You can fine-tune them later.

○ If you're using a Feelings Chart, add a fourth column entitled "Coping Strategy" and list possible techniques. (See Figure 1 for an example.)

Figure 1
Sample of a completed feelings chart:

FEELINGS CHART			
Physical Sign	Emotion	Reason	Coping Strategy
Moving fast, laughing	Happy or excited	A new video game	Stay out of people's way till I settle down
Hunched shoulders	Tense or worried	A math test tomorrow	Have Mom go over the questions with me
Fast speech and clenched teeth	Irritated or annoyed	My sister looked in my drawer	Take a deep breath, then ask her to make a deal about privacy
Lying around, not talking	Sad or down in the dumps	No one asked me to the dance	Say to myself "No one knew I was interested"; Ask one of my friends to go
Red face, rising voice volume	Angry and getting angrier	Somebody ate my Lucky Charms	Punch the punching bag to settle down; then ask Dad to take me to the store to buy my own personal box of cereal

MANAGING DISORGANIZED OR INAPPROPRIATE BEHAVIOR

As we discussed in other chapters, the disorganized or inappropriate behavior of adolescents with AS happens for many reasons. It often reflects inefficiencies in self-regulation, communication, or cognitive functioning. They may be so overwhelmed, so "hyped up," so befuddled communicatively, or so unaware of themselves and others that they violate basic norms of behavior for people their age. These violations of behavioral norms can also occur because of inadequate coping. In other words, they are so overcome by emotion that they can't manage the feelings and still keep their behavior on track. At these times, it's important for the adults to intervene.

- ○ Keep everyone safe. As noted above, when the adolescent is in an urgent situation, we don't have time to worry about the underlying reasons for the behavior. If safety is an issue for the adolescent, involve the entire team in making an emergency plan based upon a functional analysis of the adolescent and the situation.

- ○ For behaviors that are disorganized or inappropriate but not dangerous, it's still important to understand the function of the behavior. The components of functional analysis are listed in Figure 2. The functional analysis process should also be a team effort, with the adolescent as a part of the team.

- ○ After determining the function of the behavior, determine whether the adolescent has "adaptive alternatives" (also called "replacement behaviors") to the disorganized behavior. If not, teach adaptive ways of coping, as listed above.

- ○ Provide clear-cut guidelines for "desirable" or "adaptive" behavior in a given situation. You may need to memorialize these in social stories or task cards.

- ○ Provide positive consequences for any approximations of adaptive coping. Be sure to highlight the feelings/event connection and how the coping strategy helped the adolescent keep his or her behavior "in bounds."

- ○ Provide predictable and logical negative consequences when the adolescent does not use an adaptive alternative that is in his or her repertoire. For example, when Rebecca continued to rant and rave and call names, even though her father suggested that this might be a good time to have a snack and listen to music, he said, "It's not fair for the rest of us to be subjected to your insults. You have a choice—listen to music and settle down, or go to your room."

- ○ In general, try to avoid negative consequences for incompetence (that is, when the child did not have an adaptive alternative behavior or coping mechanism). At these times, teaching better ways is usually a more productive strategy.

○ Finally, remember that breakdowns in behavior or coping are inevitable for all of us. Our goal is to reduce the frequency and intensity with which these happen.

Figure 2

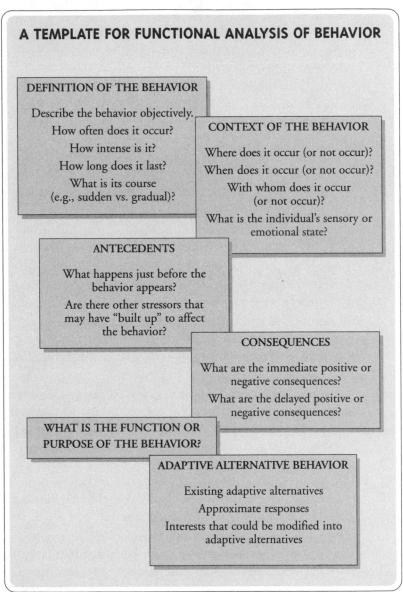

A TEMPLATE FOR FUNCTIONAL ANALYSIS OF BEHAVIOR

DEFINITION OF THE BEHAVIOR

Describe the behavior objectively.
How often does it occur?
How intense is it?
How long does it last?
What is its course
(e.g., sudden vs. gradual)?

CONTEXT OF THE BEHAVIOR

Where does it occur (or not occur)?
When does it occur (or not occur)?
With whom does it occur
(or not occur)?
What is the individual's sensory or
emotional state?

ANTECEDENTS

What happens just before the
behavior appears?
Are there other stressors that
may have "built up" to affect
the behavior?

CONSEQUENCES

What are the immediate positive or
negative consequences?
What are the delayed positive or
negative consequences?

**WHAT IS THE FUNCTION OR
PURPOSE OF THE BEHAVIOR?**

ADAPTIVE ALTERNATIVE BEHAVIOR

Existing adaptive alternatives
Approximate responses
Interests that could be modified into
adaptive alternatives

POSITIVE BEHAVIORAL SUPPORTS

Many adolescents with AS had "behavior plans" when they were younger. While behavior plans are usually helpful and well intentioned, even the title suggests that the whole process of behavioral and emotional control is more simple and one-sided than it really is. The old plans often implied, "If you behave, good things will happen. If you don't behave, there will be negative consequences." There was no mention of what the rest of us would do to establish an environment conducive to "behaving."

At this point in our understanding of AS and similar disorders, we recognize that "positive behavioral support plans" can be more helpful. This change in title reflects the change in perspective. In other words, the adolescent's everyday functioning rests as much upon what we provide as upon what the adolescent does or doesn't do. These plans consider what needs to happen in the physical and interpersonal environment, what skills need to be taught, and what other supports need to be in place in order for the individual with AS to cope and behave optimally.

Positive behavioral support plans are helpful for many adolescents with AS. Consider working with the team to create just such a plan.

FORMING AN IDENTITY AND VALUE SYSTEM

Creating an identity is one of the most important and most difficult tasks of adolescence. This creative process is one reason for peer conformity and pressure, for blue/purple/green hair, for fads, and for arguments with adults over a variety of issues. In fact, for us as human beings to understand what something truly is, we must also understand what it isn't. Adolescence is the time for "trying on" new ideas, new looks, and new feelings—if only to decide that it's "just not me." Inherent in this search for identity is a search for values—"What is okay for me to do, feel, and think?" Ironically, this is the process that most often "freaks out" parents—maybe because we remember what we did, thought, or felt as adolescents. Rest assured, though—even if the discovery of your own identity and values was a rocky road, you survived.

Finding a sense of self as an adolescent with AS is quite a variable process. For some, the process is even more baffling than for most adolescents. Problems with "seeing the shades of gray" or "understanding the big picture" can lead to confusion about "Who am I?" For other adolescents with AS, however, the issue of finding oneself doesn't come up until later, if at all. For these individuals, "identity" is just one more amorphous concept that doesn't make sense or require any attention. In the case of the latter group, it's usually easiest to let well enough alone until the issue arises at a later time.

In adolescents who do struggle with identity, there seem to be two basic questions. The first is "What kind of person am I?" The second is "What is all right for me to do?" Of course, these are also the questions that can lead to losing one's way.

SO, HOW CAN WE HELP?

Remember the first time you disagreed with your parents on something big? Remember how you felt when they attempted to lay down the law? Remember what you did in response to those feelings? Some of us were lucky enough to have parents who helped us negotiate the search for identity and values without too much rebellion. Others weren't quite so lucky, but managed to stay out of trouble anyway. Others were unlucky *and* got in trouble.

I don't pretend to have the magic answer regarding how to avoid all of the pitfalls of parenting/teaching/counseling adolescents through this search. But adolescents and their families and teachers have taught me some things that can help (and some things that can hurt). As always, effective parenting/teaching/counseling is facilitated by the presence of a strong working partnership with the adolescent.

HELPFUL ADULT BEHAVIORS

- ○ Don't take it personally, no matter what the adolescent says.
- ○ Do listen carefully. Maybe he or she has a point.
- ○ Don't attribute everything to AS. Some of it may be regular adolescence.
- ○ Don't jump to conclusions. The fact that she idolizes the rock star with pink hair and fifteen body piercings doesn't mean she's going to dye her hair and puncture her body parts.

- Don't be judgmental about his or her peers, taste in clothing and music, interests, or political beliefs (unless you are in a soundproof setting where the adolescent absolutely, positively cannot hear you).
- Observe your child's friends and peers. Listen to what they say, how they cope, and what they think of themselves.
- When asked, present your own values as simply and clearly as possible. If the adolescent is interested, provide the reasoning that backs up your opinions.
- Talk to other adults who have (or have had) children the same age. Find out what is the norm (even if it doesn't sound "normal").
- Don't freak out if your adolescent chooses a quirky identity. Remember that many adults with AS are a little out of the mainstream in one way or another. Despite their differences, they can still be happy, healthy, and productive members of society.
- KEEP YOUR SENSE OF HUMOR!

STRATEGIES THAT FOCUS ON THE ADOLESCENT

- Help him or her keep track of the big picture. Reinforce the view that he or she is a complex person with many strengths and challenges. Model the belief that others are similarly complex.
- Teach positive self-talk or self-affirmations. These have to be realistic, or the adolescent will get turned off. Try teaching self-talk like, "I'm not so good at _____, but I'm great at _____," or "I really don't want to do my math project, but after I finish I'll be able to spend the rest of the evening doing whatever I want."
- Teach and reinforce effective decision-making strategies. In particular, help the adolescent learn how to listen to both head and heart in making choices.
- Encourage conversations about values. As with other expressions of feelings, be sure to listen, listen, listen.
- Provide objective information about risky behavior. Help the adolescent with AS think about the longer-term consequences of risk taking.

A FEW WORDS ABOUT ANXIETY, DEPRESSION, AND RAGE

There are some suggestions that adolescents with AS are at increased risk for anxiety and depression. Given the load that most of them carry, it makes sense that life could seem scary or overwhelming at times. For some, the sensory, communicative, cognitive, and social demands of everyday life lead to frank anxiety or depressive disorders. For a few, the overload leads to anger and/or rageful behavior.

We hope that the increased risk of these emotional difficulties will decrease as more and more youngsters with AS receive early and intensive intervention. However, it is unlikely that early intervention alone will eliminate anxiety, depression, and rage altogether. Thus, it's important for parents and teachers to know how to handle this.

EARLY WARNING SIGNS

Sometimes it's hard to know what is the Asperger's, what is adolescence, and what is symptomatic of other emotional problems. When in doubt, seek mental health consultation. Some of the signs that indicate the need for consultation are:

- Sad or anxious mood
- Increased irritability or sudden mood changes
- Hopeless or helpless attitude
- Self-injurious or self-destructive thoughts or actions
- "Tantrums" or raging behavior
- Loss of interest in previously pleasurable activities
- Increased fearfulness or avoidance of situations that were previously mastered
- School refusal
- Drop in academic productivity or grades
- Increased forgetfulness or inattention
- Physical complaints (headache, stomachache, body aches and pains)

○ Changes in the adolescent's everyday basic functioning (eating, sleeping, energy level, involvement in home or school life)
○ Increased conflicts with others

PROFESSIONAL INTERVENTION

Intervention for adolescents with AS and emotional difficulties will be determined on the basis of individual strengths and challenges, characteristics of the environment, and the availability of services within the community. In general, it's helpful to create an intervention team that includes the adolescent, the family, the school team, and mental health professionals. Such a multidisciplinary team will be able to create a comprehensive plan that includes therapies (psychotherapy, speech/language therapy, occupational therapy), skill building (academic and social), and necessary biological interventions (such as medication).

The take-home message here is that it's virtually impossible for anyone to do the intervention alone. AS is a "24-7" challenge, and the most effective intervention considers all 24 and all 7.

A FINAL WORD

When I first began to work with adolescents with AS, the prevailing belief was that AS and emotional competence were mutually incompatible. Over the years I've discovered that we all have a journey toward emotional competence; it's just that our journeys may take different routes at different points along the way. Our task as the adults who support adolescents with AS is to help them find the ways over, under, or around the rocks that life inevitably puts in their path.

CHAPTER EIGHT

Friendship and Intimacy

A number of years ago, I worked in a psychoeducational center in suburban Atlanta. The students there were identified with a number of emotional and neurodevelopmental challenges, some of which we would now call Asperger Syndrome. Within an environment that included small class sizes, ample staff-to-student ratios, and a strong clinical team, most children and adolescents thrived. Strong connections were forged among students and between students and staff.

As winter turned to spring, the staff began to notice that "love was in the air." Or more precisely, the adolescent classrooms and therapy rooms were filled with kids talking about sex. Words and numbers became "codes" for body parts or sexual acts. Or at least so we assumed; we never could crack the code completely. Virtually every class discussion involved someone dissolving into gales of laughter because of someone else's overt or covert reference to sex or desire. Being a liberal-minded staff that had been part of the "revolutions" of the '60s and '70s, we didn't want to squelch the student's sexuality—but the sex talk and innuendo were driving the adults crazy!

Fortunately, we had a wise consultant, Stephen Nowicki, to whom we could confess our dilemma during our daily after-school debriefing. "Should we beef up our sex education offerings?" we implored. "It's not about sex. It's about intimacy," he said. Dr.

Nowicki went on to remind us that most of these students never learned about closeness through friendships with same-sex peers. They didn't have chums or pals to share their deepest, darkest secrets with. Now they had feelings of closeness, but they coincided with the adolescent rumblings of desire. They didn't know how to interpret all of this, and they assumed that closeness and warmth were sexual in nature. "Don't zero in on sex," Dr. Nowicki advised. "Help them learn about friendship."

I've probably told this story hundreds of times by now, to parents, to teachers, and to other professionals. It reminds me (and others, I hope) that we have to help all of our children learn about friendship and closeness. Not only are friendship and closeness valuable in and of themselves, but they are also the prerequisites for healthy romantic and sexual relationships in adulthood.

Adolescents with AS face numerous challenges in forming and maintaining friendships. For many, their sensory and communicative difficulties kept them from being "available" for friendships during the early and middle childhood years when others were learning "playground politics." Problems in sensory, emotional, and behavioral regulation often prevented them from participating in play dates, birthday parties, and unstructured neighborhood play. Some of them weren't especially interested in other children, preferring to pursue their own interests in their own way in their own time. Finally, to the extent that these interests were idiosyncratic and preoccupying, they may have caused a gap in the common experiences that serve as the basis for most friendships. Thus, if the adolescent with AS does become interested in friendships, he or she has a lot of catching up to do in terms of social experience.

Sometimes adolescents and their parents ask why we should push friendship skills if the individual simply isn't interested in other people. They wonder why it isn't okay to be a loner. After all, weren't Albert Einstein, Thomas Edison, and so forth? There are at least a few answers to these questions:

○ We all want to live life with the widest array of choices. If we have friendship skills, then we can make a decision about whether or not to be friends with someone else. If we don't have those skills, our choices are limited.

○ It's a lot easier to learn and practice friendship skills in school than in the workplace. If we're going to learn, school and the neighborhood usually offer the best opportunities.

○ Much of our research on adult functioning suggests that skills in social communication and relatedness are better predictors of success in the workplace than is intelligence. In a world that is increasingly based upon gathering and sharing information, it's more and more important to have some "people skills."

○ Other research suggests that connections with others are important for health and longevity. Our most vital elders are those who stay socially involved.

Even though many parents of adolescents with little social interest have come to accept that their child simply isn't "social," most also remark that their greatest fear is that their child will eventually be alone and lonely.

In fact, though, most adolescents with AS are not socially uninterested. Many want to have close friendships. Some actually do. Others strive for friendship and popularity but just don't seem to be able to pull it off. Some of these adolescents keep on trying. Others just give up.

The goal of this chapter is to discuss strategies for establishing and maintaining friendships and for gaining greater intimacy or closeness with the friends one does have. At the end, we'll touch upon the most baffling of topics—romance and (gulp) sexual relationships.

ESTABLISHING FRIENDSHIPS

What makes a friend a friend? This is hard to put into words, even for the most eloquent of adolescents. For adolescents with AS, the question can be even more confusing. In fact, many researchers and clinicians have noticed that individuals with AS and other autism spectrum disorders not only have trouble with the question but also misidentify friends. Since many adults also have difficulty with the question, let's start with a basic definition of a friend in its adolescent guise.

A friend is someone we know well. Someone we like. Someone who likes us. Someone who shares common interests, values, or experiences. Someone in whom we can confide, at least about certain things. Someone who makes us feel good about ourselves. Someone we can turn to in times of trouble. Someone who likes us even when we disagree. Someone who likes us in spite of our faults.

The themes of mutual affection, reciprocity, tolerance, and respect underlie most definitions of mature friendship. Yet these are awfully abstract concepts for adolescents with AS. It was a lot easier in early childhood when a friend was someone who had toys you liked. Or whose mom gave out good snacks. Or whose parents were friends with your parents. No wonder it's difficult for many adolescents with AS to establish friendships.

SO, HOW CAN WE HELP?

It's important to remember that friendship requires many of the communicative, regulatory, cognitive, and social skills that are so difficult for adolescents with AS. Given this, we must engage the adolescent in a working partnership around developing these skills. It's a tough road for many, and the journey won't proceed unless the adolescent finds the quest both motivating and meaningful.

CREATING OPPORTUNITIES FOR FRIENDSHIP

Once we have the adolescent's "buy in," we can begin by structuring a context in which social skills can be practiced and friendships can be formed. We must remember that many friendships (especially among boys) aren't based upon talking, but upon doing things together. These are some ideas that have worked for some adolescents:

○ Find clubs or after-school activities that relate to the adolescent's passions. Spending time with other people who enjoy the same types of things is the adolescent equivalent of parallel play in toddlers. It gives the adolescent the opportunity to observe others and, eventually, to make some connections.

○ Encourage the adolescent to invite others to join him or her for specific activities that include inherent structure. For example, it's a lot easier to interact around a few games at the bowling alley than to hang out at home.

○ When the adolescent does invite a peer to the house, try to organize the visit around a certain task or activity—coming over to check out the new Nintendo game, making cookies for the band bake sale, building a fort in the backyard, and so on.

○ Don't forget volunteer opportunities. Many adolescents with AS do much better socially with much younger or much older people. The younger people don't expect or offer sophisticated communication. The older people are able to provide communicative scaffolding when necessary. Tasks such as reading to the kindergarten class or playing piano at the senior center allow the adolescent to make connections with others. It's even more helpful if the adolescent with AS has a peer who "co-volunteers."

TEACHING SKILLS FOR FRIENDSHIP

Once we have created contexts in which interaction can occur, it's important to make sure that the adolescent recognizes the opportunities and takes advantage of them.

○ Make sure that the adolescent knows which behaviors signal that another person is available for friendship. Adolescents signal availability through actions such as: eye contact and "knowing glances," physical proximity, comments directed toward the other person, good-natured teasing, positive remarks, and offers of help.

○ Make sure that the adolescent knows how to respond in kind (assuming that he or she is interested in a friendship).

○ Teach "conversation starters" and when/where to use them.

○ Help the adolescent with AS understand the differences between good-natured teasing and harassment or bullying. Understanding these differences involves being able to step back and look at the big picture. Since this is hard for many people with AS, we may need to provide extra guidance.

○ Make sure that the adolescent understands how to carry on a two-way conversation, rather than a monologue. There are ideas about this in Chapter Three, on communication, and Chapter Nine, which deals with the "rules of the social road."

○ Help the adolescent understand that no one is the perfect friend who offers us everything we need. Most of us enjoy some people in certain situations and other people in other contexts. It's important for the adolescent with AS to understand that a friend is valuable even if he or she isn't a perfect match.

○ Encourage the adolescent to talk with someone (a parent, a teacher, a counselor, a therapist) about friendship dilemmas. "What do you think she meant when she said…?" is a legitimate question for any adolescent to ask a coach.

○ Finally, convey the message that most of us have a lot of acquaintances but not that many friends. It's important for the adolescent with AS to understand that not everyone will become a friend. This reduces the discouragement he or she feels when things don't work out.

MAINTAINING FRIENDSHIPS

Remember the first time that you realized that your best friend had another friend too? How could she be friends with both of you? Why would she want to be with one person one day and another person the next? Remember the first time you had a "fight" with your best friend? You thought you'd never speak to him again. But then there you were a day or two later, shooting hoops or laughing at the lunch table. The chances are that you learned these lessons in elementary school. You learned that friendships can last through jealousy, anger, and neglect, as long as you nurture them along the way.

Nathan really enjoys being with his friend Jake. Both enjoy rocketry and astronomy. Nathan likes to go to Jake's house and look at the stars through his telescope. He really likes building rockets and shooting them off in the field behind Jake's house. Nathan never turned down an invitation to spend time with Jake.

After a few months of this, Jake's invitations came less often and eventually stopped. He was nice to Nathan at school and he seemed interested in whatever new tidbits Nathan gleaned from the Internet. But he still didn't call. Nathan couldn't figure out what happened.

Nathan's parents, Mr. and Mrs. Marshall, had been watching all of this, but didn't want to intrude. Finally, Nathan complained that Jake wasn't friends with him anymore. Mr. and Mrs. Marshall asked him for evidence of his feelings. Then, Mr. Marshall wondered aloud if Jake knew how much Nathan liked him.

"Of course he does. I go over every time he calls!"

"Has Jake ever come over here? Have you even invited him?" Mr. Marshall asked.

"Well, no. We don't have a workshop in our basement or a field behind our house or a telescope. What would we do over here?"

Mr. and Mrs. Marshall convinced Nathan to try inviting Jake to come over. They thought of some activities that both boys might enjoy at their house. When Nathan asked, Jake eagerly accepted. When she dropped him off, Jake's mom told Mrs. Marshall that Jake had thought Nathan wasn't interested in him, only in his stuff. Nathan's failure to invite Jake to his house had made Jake think Nathan wasn't interested in him.

SO, HOW CAN WE HELP?

FEEDING A FRIENDSHIP

Many adolescents with AS have trouble making inferences about the state of mind of another person. This keeps them from seeing what another person may need or want in a relationship. We can help by teaching them how to "feed" the friendship.

○ Whenever possible, help the adolescent with AS reciprocate invitations.

○ After a get-together with a friend, ask the adolescent with AS what his or her friend did, thought, or felt during the activity. If he or she doesn't know, help him link the "data" with possible interpretations.

○ Before a get-together, help the adolescent with AS think about what the friend might want to do or eat while they're together. (I've found that getting adolescents to notice what their friends like to eat is often an easy starting place—food is concrete and usually highly motivating!)

○ If you know something exciting about the friend or his or her family, and it's okay to tell others, make sure that the adolescent with AS knows about it too. Provide as much coaching as necessary to help him or her talk with the friend about the news.

○ If the friend is going through a tough time, and it's common knowledge, coach the adolescent with AS regarding what to say (and what not to). Adolescents with AS may approach an upsetting occurrence head-on and overwhelm a friend whose strategy is to keep it at arm's length. Help the adolescent with AS see that he or she can help the friend more by giving extra attention than by asking blunt questions about the upsetting situation. Coaching not only preserves the relationship but also helps the adolescent with AS understand empathy.

○ When the adolescent with AS is going through a hard time, help him or her decide what to share with the friend and how to share it.

MANAGING CONFLICT AND DISAGREEMENT IN A FRIENDSHIP

Let's face it—managing conflict is tough for all of us (even the psychologists among us). So, it's going to be even harder for adolescents with AS. In addition to all of the developmental challenges that we've mentioned above, their conflict management skills can be compromised by their tendency to be ever so logical and to have trouble with the "grays" of life. The following suggestions offer a partial list of things we can do to help. You probably have many other strategies that you've discovered on your own.

- As part of your working partnership with the adolescent with AS, talk about what it means when people disagree.
- Try to reinforce the beliefs that make sense—such as "we can disagree and still be friends."
- Talk in a logical and data-based way about the beliefs that don't make sense. For example, if the adolescent states that a friendship is over after an argument, talk with him about what has happened when he has had disagreements with people in the past. What was the evidence that the other person held the argument against him forever? What was the evidence that the other person remained her friend?
- Listen carefully to the adolescent's interpretation of what happened. Don't move too quickly to provide another perspective. Make sure that you and the adolescent understand as much of the situation and his or her interpretation as possible.
- Once all the evidence is on the table and the adolescent lets you know that he or she is ready to try to think about things differently, help the adolescent see the other person's perspective. Sometimes it helps to make a chart with headings like: What I said, What he/she heard, What he/she said, What I heard.
- Teach about ways to clarify and repair communication: "Do you mean _____ or _____?" "I didn't get it. I thought you were saying that you wanted _____."
- Help the adolescent learn to make sincere apologies (when appropriate).
- When you're talking with the adolescent about a specific situation, be careful about bringing in examples of previous, similar situations. To some adolescents with AS, this makes them feel as if you're not listening to them. It's also hard for them to draw the parallels.
- At home or at school, practice "agreeing to disagree." Modeling the belief that people can have different values and still be friends is an important aspect of teaching adolescents to manage conflict.

○ Also, remember to teach techniques such as taking a break when tempers run too hot or bringing in a third party when compromise seems impossible.

○ Model and reinforce letting go of a conflict once it is resolved. Sometimes it helps to use the image of putting the conflict in a box and placing it on the top shelf in the attic closet. Then, if the adolescent brings it up again, remind him or her that the conflict is "on the shelf." Eventually, we would like the adolescent to use that kind of image as self-talk so that the conflict doesn't even have to be repeated aloud.

DEEPENING FRIENDSHIPS

Close friendships don't come along very often for most of us. They require not only luck (in finding someone who seems like a match) but also all of the care and feeding discussed above. In addition, though, close friendships require that intangible quality of being a soulmate and being able to know someone else's mind and heart.

Most adolescents find it perplexing to negotiate the depths of close friendship. It sometimes works out well, and adolescents find friends who can be supporters and sounding boards, while still calling them on their "junk." At other times, however, they may confide in someone who seems trustworthy, only to find out that this wasn't such a wise idea. Or they get confused by mixed messages that say, "Be my friend but don't expect too much of me." The bottom line is that almost everyone is trying to figure out closeness at this age.

SO, HOW CAN WE HELP?

Adolescents with AS often benefit from some information to guide them through the maze of close relationships. Even if they're not interested in, or comfortable with, close friendships any time soon, it will help them to have some ideas about what to do (or not do). We'll talk about some of the "what not to do" rules in Chapter Nine. For now, let's focus upon skills that we can teach, assuming that the adolescent is interested.

○ The most important skill for close friendship is listening. That means being able to listen without jumping in with experiences of one's own and being able to listen without jumping in to fix things or offer suggestions.

○ One of the hardest parts of listening is hearing about unpleasant or disturbing things. This is especially hard for adolescents with AS, since they may not know what to do with intense affect. Remind them that they don't have to fix anything. They just have to listen.

○ One of the best ways to teach listening is to model it.

○ Close friends can tolerate silence as well. Help the adolescent learn that not every silence has to be filled with words. Sometimes it's okay to just be together, doing something that you both enjoy.

○ Close friends believe in the bond between them, even when life events get in the way of being together. For example, when Sarah hadn't heard from her best friend Jane in a week, she remembered that Jane had two major projects for school and her audition for the district orchestra. Instead of calling to "yell at" Jane for not calling her, Sarah left a message for Jane—"Hope you're getting everything done. Good luck in your audition."

○ Close friends talk with each other about their feelings and life experiences. It helps the adolescent with AS to know that it is okay to talk about frustration or worries with a best friend. If it's truly a close friendship, it's also fine to talk about arguments with a parent or interest in a person of the opposite sex.

ROMANCE AND SEXUAL INTIMACY

Talk about walking with stilts on icy pavement! The only thing trickier than thinking about our own romances and sexuality is thinking about the same topics in relation to our adolescents! But we have to do it anyway. It's like being on the high diving board and not being able to climb back down—all we can do is hold our noses and jump.

Seventeen-year-old Martha wanted a boyfriend. Everywhere she looked at school kids were walking hand in hand. Every stairwell seemed to have a kissing couple. All of Martha's friends were going out with someone. Martha asked, "How can I get a boyfriend?"

Martha wasn't thrilled with her counselor's suggestion that a guy has to be a friend before he can be a boyfriend.

"You sound just like my mother," she said. "None of my friends were friends with their boyfriends first."

As she thought about the adolescents and adults around her, the counselor realized that Martha had a point. But the counselor didn't voice this agreement, because she knew that Martha could not survive the hurt of going out for a week and then being "dumped." The counselor wisely recognized that Martha needed something that wasn't as risky.

Over the next few weeks, the counselor helped Martha explore what it meant to her to have a boyfriend. What did she think "love" would feel like? Was it enough to have a guy to do things with, or did she need the romance? What were her thoughts about kissing, etc.?

It turned out that Martha wasn't really that interested in soul-searching conversations. She thought French kissing was kind of gross. What she really wanted was someone to take her to the movies and to ballgames, someone to exchange instant messages with, and someone to joke around with in the halls. Martha wanted a boy who was a friend, not necessarily a boyfriend.

SO, HOW CAN WE HELP?

When your adolescent talks about romance or boy/girlfriends or sex, find out what he or she means. Remember the little kid who asked, "Mommy, where did I come from?" Mom went into the whole birds and the bees lecture. Then the little kid replied, "That's weird. Sammy came from Chicago." We need to remember that lesson when we talk with our adolescents about romance and sexuality. Make sure that you answer the question that they're asking.

Although adolescent culture (and the associated TV/videos/ music) may not agree, it's very important for us to teach that romance and sex occur within the context of relationships. This is important for all adolescents, but it's even more critical for adolescents with AS. Their interpersonal skills and social self-esteem are such that romance is unlikely to work except in the context of a strong friendship.

MYTHS TO DISPROVE

- ○ You can go out with someone even if you've never talked with them.
- ○ You can go out with someone even if you don't know their last name.
- ○ Having a romance with a friend will ruin the friendship.
- ○ Adolescent romances last forever. If mine doesn't, something is wrong with me.
- ○ I have to have a boy/girlfriend to be popular.
- ○ I have to be sexy (or do sexy things) to be popular.
- ○ I have to be thin to get a boyfriend.
- ○ Guys/girls won't like me unless I'm pretty/handsome.

SKILLS FOR "WOOING" OTHERS

- ○ Flirting. Many adolescents (with or without AS) need help in recognizing flirtatious behavior. Unfortunately, they usually don't believe us parents when we try to "translate" for them. They're much more likely to listen to another trusted (preferably cool) adult, an older adolescent, or a peer. Other ways to help are to point out flirtatious behavior in TV shows or movies, to tell about times when you didn't recognize flirting (especially if it was with your child's other parent), or to talk about it with other children in the family. DO NOT EVER BRING IT UP IN FRONT OF HIS OR HER FRIENDS. This is a major parental sin (in the eyes of adolescents).
- ○ Smiling and looking interested (this is remarkably difficult for many adolescents with AS).
- ○ Being a good listener and remembering what the other person has talked about.
- ○ Asking about the other person's interests or experiences.
- ○ Calling on the phone/sending e-mail (be sure that the adolescent has some phone/e-mail etiquette).

○ Compliments.
○ Carefully letting others know that you're interested in a certain person (emphasize the "carefully" part).

STAYING SAFE

Most parents fear that their adolescents will be taken advantage of in relationships. This fear is often greater for parents of adolescents with developmental challenges, because we worry about their ability to see a problem coming or to get out of a risky situation once it arrives. And while the risks may seem greater for girls, our adolescent boys also need to stay safe. This isn't just about sexual behavior, but also about being led to do things that violate their own standards or the rules of their community. It also applies to the adolescent's responses to peer pressure for substance use.

As parents, teachers, and therapists, our most effective strategy is to make sure that adolescents know the risks. This isn't a time when silence is golden. Adolescents with AS are unlikely to make inferences about risk. Many are unlikely to recognize risk if it's right before their eyes. We have to provide information that is realistic, without being frightening.

Once we give sufficient information, we can work with our adolescents to make guidelines for tough (or potentially tough) situations. The most effective guidelines emerge from dialogues, rather than from dictates.

Melanie was an eighteen-year-old high school senior. In addition to her social communication challenges, she had troubling obsessions about germs and contamination. Despite these challenges, Melanie had made a remarkable adjustment to high school. She was on the debate team. She was a cheerleader. She even had a boyfriend.

Melanie came into her therapy session with a "major issue." It seems that her boyfriend had been talking with her about sex. Melanie had overcome her fear of germs well enough to tolerate kissing, but she wasn't sure about that "other stuff." The therapist was tempted to give the "no sex before marriage" talk, but she wasn't sure exactly what Melanie's "other stuff" was. She also knew that the guidelines would be more effective if Melanie took ownership for them.

As Melanie talked about the "other stuff," the therapist was able to point out that Melanie had often been disturbed by certain types of touch. The therapist also recalled Melanie's hurt feelings when other friendships and relationships hadn't turned out well. The more Melanie talked, the more she realized herself that she "couldn't handle it" if she went ahead with the "other stuff" and then the relationship didn't work out. She also realized that what her boyfriend wanted might "seriously tax" her ability to tolerate "germ exposure." Melanie ended up deciding that her personal rule was "nothing but kissing."

Melanie's ability to articulate her concerns and to arrive at a wise solution is unusual. But many adolescents can think about what rules work for them, if we can just tolerate our own anxiety as they work through the process.

For adolescents who can't come up with their own set of wise personal rules, we need to make sure that they have the skills to recognize and avoid "set ups," to say "no" in the face of peer pressure, and to refrain from taking advantage of others.

And, by the way, once rules are established, adolescents with AS are less likely to break those rules than adolescents without AS. There are times when the "black and white" thinking of AS is a real comfort to parents, teachers, and therapists!

RECOGNIZING AND AVOIDING SET UPS

The basic rule of thumb for any adolescent: If somebody tells you to do something that you think is against the rules, stop and think. Ask yourself if harm could come of it. Count to ten. Ask yourself the question again. Even if you don't think of any specific harm, don't do whatever it is. If it's against the rules, you're better off avoiding it.

SAYING "NO" IN THE FACE OF PEER PRESSURE

For many adolescents with AS, saying "no" in the face of peer pressure is not as difficult as it is for adolescents without AS. They are less concerned (or less aware) of the social disapproval that may come as a result.

For the adolescent with AS who also wants to be popular, saying "no" can be a tremendous problem. Unable to step back and realize that a true friend will respect someone who sticks to his or her values, the adolescent with AS may be afraid that saying "no" will risk the friendship. This is when we can prevail upon the adolescent's strong logic to do a "pros and cons" list (on paper or in his or her head). We may need to plant the seed (without preaching) that a friend isn't worth keeping if he or she doesn't respect your preference.

The other trick to teach adolescents is that they can use "little white lies" to escape peer pressure. Most adolescents with AS are notoriously poor liars, so it takes some work to teach them to do this. But remarks like "I'm allergic to beer" or "Cigarettes make me throw up" or "I have to be home in ten minutes" can be extremely useful when peer pressure is high.

TAKING ADVANTAGE OF OTHERS

Many adolescents with AS have been lucky enough to grow up around people who make allowances for their idiosyncrasies. Kind peers will play the game that the child with AS chooses, because they recognize that shifting gears is tough. Others may not take offense at insults, because they recognize that the child with AS didn't mean it the way it sounded.

As wonderful as it is for others to make allowances, it does have a disadvantage. The child or adolescent with AS doesn't learn that his or her behavior may be forcing other people to do things that they don't like.

There are at least three ways we can help:

○ Insisting on our own way, at least some of the time, and helping the adolescent with AS cope with disappointment.
○ Letting siblings and peers know that they don't always have to give in.

○ Teaching the adolescent with AS that "'No' means 'no' and 'stop' means 'stop'"

A FINAL WORD

Some adolescents have the notion that being popular is "the be-all and the end-all." Ironically, some of these adolescents don't make the connection between being popular and being a good friend to other people. Others don't see the value of friendship of any kind. Others have friends or boy/girlfriends, but compromise themselves or their values.

If we can accomplish nothing else in this friendship domain, our goal should be to equip our adolescents with the skills to be friends and to be loved without losing themselves in the process. Even if they're not interested in friendships now, it helps to provide them with a framework. Because none of us wants our children to be lonely.

CHAPTER NINE

The Rules of the (Social) Road

Joanna's grandmother, Mrs. Flynn, had been laid off from her job at a factory in another state. She was taking advantage of the time off by visiting her grandchildren. It was an exciting time for Joanna and her sisters, because they weren't accustomed to having such long, leisurely visits with Mrs. Flynn.

One summer afternoon, Joanna, her sisters, her mother, and her grandmother did their errands and then went to meet Joanna's father for lunch. Mr. Flynn was already outside, enjoying the summer day. From across the street, Joanna called out, "Hi, Dad! We just took Grandma to the unemployment office! Now it's time for lunch!"

Mr. Flynn and both Mrs. Flynns gave her "the look."

"What? What did I do?"

Her mother muttered, "You shouldn't yell out that your grandmother is unemployed!"

Joanna was baffled. "Why not? It's the truth," she thought.

Joanna had violated one of those unwritten "rules of the road"—those guidelines that many people just seem to know and that other people learn the hard way. Unfortunately, individuals with Asperger Syndrome and other autism spectrum disorders often learn the rules the hard way.

THE RULES OF THE (SOCIAL) ROAD

"What I wanted . . . were rules I could carry around with me that applied to all situations, regardless of context."

—Donna Williams, *Somebody Somewhere.*

Donna Williams, an eloquent author who also has an autism spectrum disorder, captured the dilemma that faces many adolescents with AS. They wonder: "What are these rules that everyone else seems to 'just know'?" They question, "What will happen to me if I follow these rules? What will happen to me if I don't?"

Most of us learn the rules of the road by watching and listening to other people. Beginning in preschool, we notice who does and says what. We notice what happens to them as a result. We try to imitate the behaviors that seem to produce consequences we like and to avoid the behaviors that produce consequences we don't like. And if we happen to miss one of those connections, somebody is sure to tell us. Even as early as preschool we start to form a set of internalized rules for behavior. And although we can't always manage to follow those rules "in the moment," we do have a budding framework.

Our growing framework of rules is not just for "right" and "wrong" in the moral sense. It's also for "right" and "wrong" in the social sense. As children move into elementary school and beyond, they're able to take the rules that were initially based upon the consequences for a specific behavior and expand them to cover a variety of situations and people. This process of generalization is very helpful to parents and teachers, because it spares us the chore of reminding children what not to do in every conceivable situation. Their growing social awareness (or social cognition) also allows them to feel empathy for others and to treat them with respect and consideration.

For adolescents with AS, social awareness may not be as well developed. Numerous obstacles may have prevented them from learning the rules of the road. When the other preschoolers were learning playground politics, the child with AS was still trying to run across the schoolyard without running into people and things. When the other kids in first grade were noticing who liked to eat what, the child with AS was working hard to tolerate the noise, smells, and touches within the busy classroom. When other third graders were beginning to make inferences about what they read and how people felt, the child with AS was still quite literal in his or her interpretation of books and life.

Temple Grandin, Ph. D., has spoken many times of her confusion about the "rules." She points out that many of them are incredibly illogical. If one of the basic tenets of our society is tell the truth, why are little white lies okay? If speeding is illegal, why do so many fine upstanding citizens practice it every day? Dr. Grandin is speaking for many of our adolescents with AS when she comments about the nonsensical nature of all of this.

It's true that many of these rules don't make logical sense, at least within the strict definition of "logical." Yet we all know that there are many consequences of breaking the rules of the social road. Some of the consequences are relatively minor. Others can be troubling or even dangerous.

SO, HOW CAN WE HELP?

As Donna Williams wrote, it's important to know the "rules" if one is to make wise choices about behavior. Knowing the rules also allows us to function independently and safely. Teaching adolescents (with or without AS) the rules of the road is one way to ensure that they know what to do, even when they don't do it.

As the grownups, we may face some resistance from our adolescents when we try to teach them these rules. It may be hard to get the working partnership to kick in here, because many adolescents with AS simply don't see the value in talking about "all that boring stuff." This is a time when we have to be patient— remember that "ripeness is all." This is a time when we have to think the way they think. Like most of us, they are most interested in the feelings and behavior of others when there is a direct impact on them. For example, one boy told me last week that he really didn't care that much about being popular, so it didn't matter what other kids thought about him. When a female classmate kicked him in the groin because he called her an idiot, he suddenly became a little more interested in the rules of the road. "Why did she do that? Kids call other kids idiots all the time."

When we face resistance about teaching the rules of the road, it's important to help the adolescents see the relevance for them. Then, we'll be more likely to achieve a working partnership around this issue.

Knowing the rules is one aspect of our task. Another aspect is helping the adolescent with AS understand why the rules are the rules. Since many have trouble taking the perspectives of others, they may not recognize the feelings and thoughts that make the rules so important. Teaching empathy and "perspective taking" is even harder than teaching the rules, however. It requires us to make inferences about the mental states of others (Theory of Mind). It requires us to understand the "shades of gray" in a situation. Neither of these is easy for most adolescents with AS. Often we're most successful in teaching perspective taking when we focus first on what the adolescent likes and doesn't like. Then we can build this into a "mental map" of others.

Finally, we can help our adolescents by admitting that some rules just have to be followed. No matter how illogical. No matter how much of a pain. And why? "Because you'll get in big trouble if you don't follow them."

THE RULES THAT GRANDMOTHER TAUGHT . . . AND A MODERN INTERPRETATION

Maybe you didn't learn the rules of the road from Grandmother. But you learned them from someone, somehow. We should make sure that our adolescents know these rules and the basic reasons for them. The list below certainly is an incomplete one. Feel free to add or subtract rules as needed for your family and community. The take-home message here is that adolescents with AS may not have learned them in the traditional way and that we have to teach them.

One caution is in order: There are a *lot* of rules. We could never teach all of them, especially in a single sitting. And no adolescent likes lectures. These rules are most successfully taught in natural settings and in the context of a working partnership. That said, these are some of the rules to teach. (By the way, some adolescents

enjoy making cartoons or skits of these rules and sharing them
with others.)

- Don't stare. (It makes people uncomfortable. It can give
  them the wrong idea.)
- Don't ask someone's age, weight, family income, price of
  their home, or how much they paid for their clothes.
  (This can be embarrassing for some people. Especially if
  they're not happy with whatever you asked about.)
- Don't tell someone else's age, weight, family income, etc.
  (Same reasons.)
- Don't comment about someone's body or body parts.
  (Again, this embarrasses a lot of people, especially if they
  think that part of their body is a problem.)
- Don't make negative comments about someone's race,
  ethnic origin, or religion. (In our culture, most of us
  believe that it's important to respect and value differences
  among people. Negative comments about race, ethnic origin, or religion are often considered bigoted and narrow-
  minded. They bring negative attention to the "commenter"
  and can risk relationships.)
- Don't make negative comments about someone's clothing
  or hairstyle, even if they ask. (Everyone has their own taste
  in clothes or hairstyle. Besides, they might already feel bad
  about what they look like.)
- Don't call other people names, even if everyone else is
  doing it. (This can hurt someone's feelings. Plus, you don't
  want others to call you names.)
- Don't touch others without their permission. (This can be
  a violation of personal space and make people uncomfortable. Also, other people may have sensory issues similar to
  your own.)
- Respect personal space. (Same as above.)
- Don't walk or stand between people who are already having a conversation. (This is rude. It suggests that you
  believe their interaction with each other is unimportant.)
- Our culture expects people in greater authority to be
  treated with respect. (People in authority include anyone
  older than you—parents, teachers, counselors, family

members, neighbors, clerks in stores, etc. When you're an adult, people in authority may be your age, but have more power—for example, a boss.)

○ **When speaking to people who are older than you or in authority, use a calm and respectful tone of voice.** (Older people expect and deserve respect, even if they haven't treated you in a similar manner. Besides, disrespectful behavior is the fastest route to the principal's office or discipline room!)

○ **When speaking to people who are older than you or in authority, avoid the use of slang.** ("Duh," "whatever," or "What was it about ___ that you didn't understand?" may be the way to talk around peers. It can get you in trouble with adults.)

○ **Try to look at other people when you're talking with them.** (This lets them know that you're interested. It lets them know when you need their attention. It lets them know if you don't understand. It lets you know if they don't understand.)

○ **If it's too much to make eye contact and talk at the same time, think of eye contact like punctuation. Use it like a capital letter to say that a sentence is starting. Use it to emphasize something important. Use it like a period, question mark, or exclamation point to show that you've finished your thought.** (People may not know when you're starting and finishing if you don't give them non-verbal signals.)

○ **Don't swear or make obscene gestures.** (Other kids may be able to get away with it, but you probably can't because it's hard for you to know when and where to do it or when to stop.)

○ **Don't tattle, unless physical, sexual, or emotional harm is involved.** (If someone else breaks a rule and it doesn't hurt someone, stay out of it. Other kids don't like tattlers and complainers.)

○ **"People who live in glass houses shouldn't throw stones."** (All of us have some faults. It's not a good idea to make judgments about anyone.)

RULES ABOUT EMPATHY AND PERSPECTIVE TAKING

It may seem strange to make rules about empathy and perspective taking. As some parents worry, "I don't want him to be considerate because it's the rule. I want him to be considerate because he feels that way naturally." For adolescents with AS, though, feelings of empathy and consideration may not be "natural," at least not yet. We have to give them the skills to behave empathically or considerately, even when they don't completely "get it." By behaving in a considerate way, they'll increase the chances that others will view them as empathic and sensitive. The resulting behavior of others will be a natural reinforcer for the adolescent's efforts. Finally, especially if we pick "teachable moments," the adolescent with AS will begin to understand the perspective of others.

Dave is a fourteen-year-old ninth grader at the local high school. For years, his parents had been teaching him such rules of the road as "Don't stare" and "Don't make comments about the bodies of others." These rules had come in handy, as Dave was quite interested in his female classmates and their increasingly attractive faces and bodies. His rule-bound nature and his parents' instructions had kept him from showing his interests aloud and in public.

One day, one of the "top-three most attractive" girls in the class was bending over to put something in her backpack as Dave stood talking with a buddy. He saw her bra and the top of her breasts. To his credit, Dave turned away and pretended that nothing had happened.

He later confided in his father. Mr. Miller was duly impressed with Dave's behavior. He was even more thrilled with what came next. Dave told him, "I turned away because I didn't want her to see me see her. That could have really embarrassed her."

Mr. Miller praised Dave. As he later told his wife, "I thought he'd never learn to feel another person's feelings. But he's really starting to get it!"

Rules about empathy and perspective taking include many of the rules that Grandmother taught us (listed above). Adolescents, families, and teachers have also found the rules and reasons below to be helpful.

○ **Respect the feelings and moods of others.** (I have different moods. Other people do, too. We all have the right to feel our feelings.)

○ **No matter how I feel, it's important to follow the Golden Rule—treat others as I want to be treated.** (Everyone has the right to his or her feelings and opinions. No one has the right to treat others poorly.)

○ **Other people like to be heard.** (When I talk on and on and don't give others a chance to talk, I can hurt their feelings. What's more, they might not want to be around me anymore. And . . . if I listen, I might find out something new.)

○ **Different people care about or get bothered by different things.** (Some of my pet peeves are different from those of my classmates. Everybody is unique. That's okay.)

○ **Even when I don't agree with or understand a person's feelings, I should remember that their feelings are important.** (I know how I feel when someone tells me that my feelings are foolish.)

○ **No matter what, I shouldn't laugh, make a joke, or interrupt when someone else is upset.** (This gives others the message that I don't care about their feelings.)

RULES FOR SENDING THE MESSAGES YOU WANT TO SEND

Sometimes it's hard to know how one's behavior affects the opinions of others. We may not be aware of what we're doing. We may not notice that our behavior is violating the norms for the situation. We may not know that the other person is particularly sensitive to certain messages. This aspect of social awareness is difficult for many people, especially individuals with AS.

Teaching adolescents about the messages they send is important for many reasons. It reduces the chances that they'll offend others. It lessens the likelihood of getting in with the "wrong" crowd. It decreases the risk of victimization.

As with any other attempt to teach our adolescents about life, we have to ensure their buy in. Remember when your parents told you that going bra-less would make other people think you were cheap? Remember when they said that your long hair and mustache would make others think you were irresponsible? How did you feel about those lectures? Ideally, we need to convey the "rules" below in a nonjudgmental manner, without lecturing. But we also have to stand our ground when the adolescent's behavior is risky or reckless. So . . . here are some rules to teach.

- Long hair (on boys or girls) is okay if it's clean and well kept. (Our hair is very noticeable evidence of what we think of ourselves. Relatively neat hair suggests that we're making efforts to be presentable.)
- Showers and deodorant are essential. (Even if the dirt or smell doesn't bother us, it is likely to bother others. Also, it sends a message about what we think of ourselves.)
- Clothes should be changed at least every day. (Same as above.)
- Even if you don't care that much about clothes and belongings, try to match the basic styles with the clothing of classmates. (If no one else is carrying Elmo lunch boxes, think about getting yourself a plain one. If the other guys are wearing baggy T-shirts, don't wear form-fitting ones. Being out of step with styles can draw negative attention to you.)
- Make sure that your clothing fits in with school rules. (Schools have rules about things like belly shirts and "Co-Ed Naked" T-shirts because they want students to be thinking about schoolwork, not bodies.)
- Make sure that your clothing fits your body. (Like hair, clothing sends a message about how much you care about yourself.)
- Don't wear "provocative" clothing to school. (Belly shirts, see-through shirts, spaghetti straps, and short shorts can make others think you're showing off your body. Besides, who can do schoolwork if she's worrying about falling straps?)
- Don't brag. (No matter how good you are at something, it's important to be humble. Nobody likes a know-it-all.)
- Keep the promises you make. And try not to make a promise that you can't keep. (Keeping promises is basic to

trust. And if you don't keep your promises, others may not keep their promises to you.)

○ **Keep the secrets that others tell you.** (Keeping secrets is one of the basic elements of trust in a relationship.)

○ **The only exception to this is when someone is in danger.** (If a friend tells you something that makes you think that he/she is at risk, tell the friend that you need to tell a trusted adult. If the friend refuses, and you believe that there is a real risk, tell a parent or counselor anyway. It's better to be safe than sorry.)

○ **Don't trash other people.** ("Trashing" means criticizing, usually in a mean way. Whether in public, on the phone, or on the Internet, trashing others can come back to haunt you.)

○ **NEVER EVER give out your name, address, or phone number when you're online.** (No matter how nice the person on the other end seems, it's risky to give out personal information to someone you've never seen.)

○ **NEVER EVER agree to meet someone whom you've only known online. If someone online urges you to do this, tell your parents.** (Again, too much risk.)

○ **Don't order anything online or by telephone without parental permission.** (Again, too many risks).

○ **NEVER EVER give information to telemarketers, without speaking with your parents first.** (Ditto the reasons above.)

○ **Don't forward e-mail from one friend to another friend without the first friend's permission.** (This is the same as keeping secrets and promises.)

○ **Treat people the way you want to be treated.**

HARASSMENT AND THREATS

MAKING SURE THAT YOU DON'T HARASS OR THREATEN

Marty and his friends were fooling around while their computer teacher talked with another adult. The guys were joking and teasing about who liked which girl in their cluster. One of the other guys

said, "Marty, you love Suzie. I bet you dream every night about kissing her." Marty made a fake growl, pulled his pencil-laden fist back
as though to punch or stab, and said, "I'm gonna kill you!"

The teachers looked around just as Marty raised his arm and
spoke his words. The next thing Marty knew, he was in the principal's office for making threats against others. The principal
reminded Marty that the school had a "zero tolerance policy"
regarding threats and harassment.

Marty was totally confused. By his reckoning, he and the guys
had just been fooling around.

Most of us can probably remember similar instances in our adolescence. Even as adults, we've probably made statements like, "I'm
gonna kill you" or "I'm so mad I could strangle her!" In our experiences, though, it was unlikely that someone would get in trouble
for this type of behavior.

Times have changed, however. Because of increasing difficulties
with threatening, harassing, or dangerous behaviors in our schools,
many states and school districts have adopted "zero tolerance" for
behavior that could potentially endanger others. These policies have
been met with mixed feelings. It's easy to criticize the principal who
expels a six-year-old who brings a "weapon" to school if the weapon
is a water gun. We can become impatient with a staff member who
reports the "harmless fooling around" of adolescents, especially of
an adolescent who also has a social communication disorder such as
AS. On the other hand, it's equally common to criticize the faculty
that didn't take action about an adolescent who goes on to shoot
people in school after weeks or months of threats and violent essays.
Unfortunately, threatening and dangerous words and actions seem
to be a part of adolescent life, and we need to equip our schools'
staff members with ways to keep everyone safe.

Since it's unlikely that the "safe school zone" laws or "zero tolerance" policies will disappear in the near future, it is absolutely
imperative for us to teach our adolescents how to interact and/or
express feelings in more acceptable ways. In other words, even if he
doesn't really mean it when he says, "I'm gonna kill you," he still
can't say it. Here are some rules to teach.

○ **"No" means "no," and "Stop" means "stop."** (Friends and boy/girlfriends need to know that you will respect their wishes. Don't push somebody to do something he or she finds uncomfortable. This is always important, but becomes even more so in the dating scene.)

○ **Don't take weapons (real or play) to school. Know what your school considers a weapon.** (This is a certain way to get yourself in the principal's office or worse. Don't even be tempted to test the rule.)

○ **Don't talk about killing, physical aggression, or property destruction in public, no matter who else is saying it.** (These words can be interpreted as threats or harassment.)

○ **If you have violent or destructive thoughts or feelings, talk with your parents or counselor about them.** (These are important feelings to share with a trusted adult. It's important to keep you and everybody else safe.)

> **NOTE TO PARENTS:** If your adolescent confides these feelings to you, it is critical to seek mental health consultation immediately.
>
> **NOTE TO TEACHERS/COUNSELORS:** If an adolescent confides these feelings, inform him or her that this is something that is important to share with parents. Ask if he/she would like you to speak with parents alone or with him/her. ✸

○ **Try expressing anger and frustration in more acceptable ways.** (Remember, it's fine to feel negative feelings. It becomes a problem only when you express them in ways that frighten others.)

○ **Be careful about expressing affection. This is something to reserve for people you know very well.** (Many people are put off by physical affection from folks they consider acquaintances. They become very uncomfortable with expressions of love, frequent compliments about their appearance, or premature invitations to "go out." For some people, this feels like sexual harassment.)

○ **Similarly, by middle school, stay away from hugging folks of the opposite sex, except for your family or your mutually-agreed-upon boy/girlfriend.** (Same problems as above.)

○ **Don't tell sexual jokes in public, no matter what your friends are doing. Save these for sleepovers or camping trips with your buddies.** (Sexual jokes make many people feel very uncomfortable. They can be considered sexual harassment.)

○ **Be prepared for the consequences of breaking these rules.** Even if you "didn't mean anything by it," your school administrator is supposed to make sure that everyone is safe.

The Bottom Line on Threats and Harassment

Playing around with this is not worth the hassle. If you're not just playing around, you need to talk with a trusted grownup ASAP. ☀

RESPONDING TO THREATS AND HARASSMENT

I remember when I was a teenager. All the guys liked the girls who laughed at the dirty jokes. If a girl didn't laugh, the guys called her a prude. They also called her a prude if she didn't go "parking" with her steady guy on Saturday night. Sometimes the steady guy threatened to break up if she didn't at least go to "first base."

Times have changed. Now a PG-13 movie shows more sex and violence than middle class kids knew about during the 1950s and '60s. Many adolescents know more about sexuality, violence, and substance abuse than we knew when we graduated from college. But today's culture takes a dim view of threats and harassment, sexual or otherwise. In fact, most of what the guys said back then would be considered sexual harassment now.

But, kids still want to avoid being called "prudes," "sissies," "Mama's boys," or whatever the current terminology is for folks who are offended by violent or sexual talk/actions. How can our adolescents (with or without AS) protect themselves from victimization without losing the esteem of their peers? What are acceptable ways to respond to words and actions that make them uncomfortable?

○ **Know the facts and the slang.** (Adolescents can unwittingly set themselves up for teasing and harassment just by responding innocently to the current lingo.)

- If someone says something that makes you uncomfortable, don't react dramatically. (Reactions, especially dramatic ones, just reinforce the teasing or harassment.)
- If you do react, make it unremarkable. (This is a great time to use that word "Whatever" in a bored tone of voice and walk away.)
- If they still don't stop, make an excuse to get away. (This is a perfect opportunity to use a little white lie, such as "Mr. Jones (the principal) just called me down to his office.")
- Make sure you keep your parents and/or counselor informed of any teasing or harassment. (This is not the same as tattling! You're not looking to get the other kids in trouble. You're asking someone to help you.)
- If someone threatens you, get away as soon as you can. Do not threaten back. (Keeping safe is the first priority. After you get away, tell a trusted adult as soon as possible.)
- If someone (adult or kid) makes sexual advances or "talks dirty," get away as soon as possible. Then tell a trusted adult as soon as possible. (Again, staying safe is the number-one priority.)
- If your boy/girlfriend makes sexual advances that make you uncomfortable, get away as quickly as possible, even if you have to tell a lie. (Physical affection and sexual behavior are supposed to happen in the context of a mutual and trusting relationship. If you're uncomfortable, something is wrong. Talk with a trusted adult about it.)
- If someone abuses you physically, sexually, or emotionally, tell a trusted adult AS SOON AS POSSIBLE. (This isn't tattling. This is keeping yourself safe.)

NOTE TO PARENTS: If your adolescent reports such abuse to you, seek mental health consultation immediately.

NOTE TO PROFESSIONALS: If an adolescent makes such a report, follow the mandated reporting guidelines in your community.

- If someone approaches you online, tell your parents ASAP.

CONFIDENTIALITY IN COUNSELING AND PSYCHOTHERAPY

Most counseling/psychotherapy relationships are based on the belief that discussions in the session are confidential. Technically, any parent of a child under 18 is entitled to information that a therapist learns in a session. But most parents and therapists agree that the therapist need not divulge every detail or even every single concern that the adolescent voices. An important exception to this is when a client (adult, adolescent, or child) confides something that indicates that he/she or someone else may be in danger.

Some adolescents hesitate to tell their therapists about sexual or violent feelings, thoughts, or actions, because they fear that the therapists will "tell." In practice, though, most therapists talk with a client before telling others this kind of information. Unless danger is imminent, they don't race off immediately to tell the parents or school, because they want the adolescent to feel that it's safe to confide. A more common solution is for the therapist to "level" with the adolescent about the risks and then to make a plan about how the two of them can make sure that parents and other important adults know what they need to know in order to be helpful.

Safety always comes first.

A FINAL NOTE

The rules of the road can go on and on. And they probably change almost as often as the sun rises. None of us has perfect social awareness. None of us shows sensitive, empathic, and considerate behavior in every single situation. We're all on the journey of trying to do the best we can with what we've got.

Our best hope for being helpful in the working partnership with our adolescents is to equip them with the knowledge of the "rules" and to provide a listening ear when anything goes awry. With their skills and our support, their journey down the road of life is more likely to be a successful one.

CHAPTER TEN

Getting Ready for the Real World

The journey of a thousand miles starts with a single step.
—Chinese Proverb

When my son was only a day old, a friend called from across the country. We shared our excitement about the wonder of baby boys, hers and mine in particular. Then she said, "And isn't it incredible that this sweet, soft baby boy will grow up into a big, HAIRY *MAN?!*" I burst into tears. I had just gotten him. How could I think about him becoming a man so soon?

How fast they all grow up! Even those difficult and "never-ending" phases pass so quickly. It's really true that the day they are born is their first step away from us and our homes.

ASPERGER SYNDROME AND THE REAL WORLD

This book is about journeys. Our journeys as parents, teachers, or counselors are those of walking with our children toward adulthood. We bask in their newfound sophistication and accomplishments, even as we worry about the next step. Each skill we teach, each bit

162

of wisdom we provide has the ultimate goal of helping our children move toward happy and healthy lives in the "real world." We teach for the benefit of our kids, but also to soothe our own anxiety—maybe if we give them a rule and a reason for everything, we have a guarantee that they will be fine.

But for parents, teachers, and other helpers of adolescents with Asperger Syndrome, the task feels even more urgent. There are legitimate concerns about self-sufficiency, about judgment, about relationships, and about "fitting in." The dawning of adolescence makes time seem so short—with so much to accomplish.

Adolescents with AS seem to have many of the same concerns that trouble their so-called "typical" peers. Relationships, college, careers, sex, drugs/smoking/eating, and (sometimes) social or political causes are paramount issues. And though the motto for the current generation appears to be "Whatever," don't believe for a minute that they are really that blasé. One minute they can't wait to be living in their own apartment with their own (fast) car; the next, they wish they could curl up on the couch and have Mom serve them powdered-sugar doughnuts and chocolate milk. One minute they know the answers to all the world's ills; the next, they need their father to tell them whether to go to the dance or go snow-tubing with the guys.

For some adolescents with AS, feelings about the journey toward the "real world" are quite similar to those of everyone else. For a few, though, this journey is full of anxiety—"How will I know how to write a check?" "What do you do at work, anyway?" "How will I manage at college when I can't manage my assignment book at home?" For some, the anxiety is compounded by very real challenges in learning, organization, and communication.

Throughout this book, we've talked about ways to use a working partnership between adolescents and adults to ease the passage through adolescence. We've also talked about AS as a result of a brain with "glitches," rather than as a disability. Yet, as we consider entry into adulthood, it is in the area of disability law that we often find the supports and protections that our sons and daughters need. In this chapter, we'll talk about preparing for the passage into adulthood—the "real world." And we'll confront the reality that, at least for some individuals, AS represents a disability that requires special considerations.

WHAT TO TELL, WHOM TO TELL, AND WHEN TO TELL IT

Many parents and adolescents ask how much they should disclose about AS. They worry about how the information may influence what people think. They also worry about what people will think if they don't have a framework in which to interpret the adolescent's behavior. What to tell, whom to tell, and when to tell it is ultimately a personal and family decision. Here are some of the thoughts that other families and adolescents have shared with me over the years.

INFORMATION FOR THE ADOLESCENT

Many adolescents already know that they have AS. Some were given this information at the time of diagnosis. For others, they learned of the diagnosis after repeated frustrating encounters with everyday life.

Other adolescents don't know about AS. Their parents may have chosen not to "label" their child's difficulties, for fear of creating a stigma. Other families simply don't think in terms of labels and syndromes; they just take people as they are, a day at a time. Some families haven't talked with their adolescent about AS because the diagnosis was recent.

While the decision of whether and what to tell an adolescent ultimately resides with the parents, there are a few reasons to be direct.

o **Having a label sometimes reduces fear.** One eleven-year-old returned to school on the day after his visit with the neurologist, carrying something in a "plain brown wrapper." When it was time for his session with the therapist, he pulled out a copy of Tony Attwood's book, turned to the "Frequently Asked Questions" section, and said, "This helps so much. I thought I was crazy. Now I know that it's just AS."

o **Having a label can reduce self-blame.** Adolescents with AS, like many individuals with learning challenges, have heard frequent messages about trying harder, listening more carefully, thinking before they act or speak, and being respectful. Even their best efforts, though, haven't always led to success. Having a label can reassure them that their "failures" aren't just a function of being lazy or rude.

○ **Having a label allows the adolescent to learn what has worked for others.** Once they learn that others also have something called Asperger Syndrome, they can begin to think in terms of using their considerable strengths to compensate for their glitches.

Once a family decides to provide a diagnosis for the adolescent, it's important to do so in a respectful and optimistic manner. I usually start with something like this, "Like everybody else, you have a brain that is good at some stuff and not so good at other things. Your brain works great for _____. It doesn't work as efficiently for _____."

Then, I wait for the adolescent's reaction. Some are ready to ask more questions. Others need to mull over the information. When the adolescent is ready (and the parents have given the okay), we move toward giving these inefficiencies a name.

The take-home message that I try to impart is this: "Everybody has glitches. Your glitches happen to have a name, Asperger Syndrome. Knowing a name for your glitches puts you ahead of many of us. Knowing the name gives you a shortcut—it shows where your glitches might be and what you can do to get around them. Knowing the name also gives your parents, teachers, and counselors ideas about ways to help. But remember—you aren't Asperger Syndrome. You are a person first, and a person with AS second."

INFORMATION FOR THE SCHOOL OR COLLEGE

What schools know about a given student depends upon a whole host of factors, only some of which are specific to AS. Extent of educational challenge, age at diagnosis, the school's prior experience with AS, and the student's social and emotional profile are but a few of these factors.

Some adolescents with AS have already been identified as individuals in need of special educational services, usually by virtue of difficulties in communication or learning that were identified earlier in life. Even if the diagnosis of AS was not part of the original picture, the educational team has been aware of processing difficulties that interfered with the student's academic and/or social success. For these students, adding the AS information is relatively simple. Our main task is to ensure that the school team is aware of the particular challenges that AS presents for adolescent life at school and at home.

For students who have not demonstrated frank educational handicaps, the decision to disclose the AS diagnosis may not be as clear-cut. Some families fear the creation of a "self-fulfilling prophecy." They worry that teachers will have different expectations if they learn about the AS diagnosis. Some adolescents worry that this disclosure will make them "different." Certainly, every situation is unique, and the decision to disclose may depend as much on what will happen if you don't tell, as on what will happen if you do. One problem with not telling is that the student's behavior may be interpreted as "willful," "rude," "disrespectful," "lazy," or "spoiled" instead of as a function of very real brain inefficiencies. Another problem is that withholding the information may prevent the student from accessing support services. Some students with AS require modifications of standardized tests (such as SATs) that can only occur if a diagnosis is disclosed. For these reasons, many families come down on the side of telling. In the final analysis, though, the adolescent and his or her family must do the "pros and cons" list for their unique situation in their unique community.

As the adolescent approaches college application time, this question usually arises again. The decision regarding what to write on the college or trade-school application is just as complex as the decision to tell anybody else. A few additional factors to consider:

o Will the student benefit from access to a "Learning Skills Center" or something similar at college?

o Will modifications of course requirements be necessary (e.g., taking oral exams instead of writing in a blue book, having extra time for tests)?

o Will the student need additional supports (such as lecture tapes or copies of the lecture notes)?

o Will the student benefit from a specialized mentor or advisor, rather than simply someone from the faculty advisor pool?

○ Will the student benefit from a single room or housing in the "quiet dorm" as a function of sensory or social factors?

The greater the need for these modifications of the college or trade-school environment, the higher the priority of talking with the college about AS.

INFORMATION FOR EMPLOYERS

Sam (our teenage driver in Chapter One) had worked at the local supermarket for four years. He was a competent bagger, complimented by customers and cashiers alike for his quick and safe handling of delicate items. He was never late for work, and he willingly took on those dreaded Saturday evening shifts.

Wanting to reward Sam for his diligence, the store manager began to encourage him to learn the cashier's role. Every time Sam got behind the cash register, he became anxious and irritable. Interpreting Sam's behavior as simply a lack of confidence, the manager kept encouraging him to try again. But each encouragement just left Sam feeling more panicky. He didn't want to have to deal directly with customers, especially when they had been waiting in a long line! But he also didn't want to make his manager mad.

After talking with his parents, Sam decided to tell his manager about AS. He told him that he liked bagging because there were "rules" for packing a "good bag." He got to be around familiar people (his fellow employees), but he didn't have to deal directly with customer emotions. He made a good wage, and he went home without worries. "Career advancement" just made him nervous.

Sam's manager appreciated the information. He also appreciated Sam's promptness and responsibility on the job. The manager no longer pushed Sam to take on more responsibility. He rewarded Sam by giving him his preferred shifts and predictable, though small, raises.

Sam kept the bagging job through his postgraduate high school year. When he was ready to move on to something full-time, his manager gave him a glowing recommendation.

In Sam's case, providing information to the employer became necessary because he was doing so well that the supervisor wanted to promote him to greater responsibilities.

In other cases, it's important to provide information in order to ensure that the supervisor provides the kind of supervision that leads to on-the-job success.

When Tim (our bookstore worker in Chapter Three) received a detailed list of things to do from his boss, one of the items was "straighten the books on the shelves." Tim tried to follow this instruction, but discovered that he didn't know exactly what his boss meant. Did she mean to make sure that all the books were standing up straight? This was so hard to do with used paperbacks. Or did she mean to pull all the books to the front of the shelves, so their spines were lined up? Or should he push everything to the back of the shelves? Tim became so concerned with these questions that he stayed up late at night worrying. He missed a few days of work because he slept through his alarm.

Tim's boss was surprised that he missed two days of work without calling in. She called Tim's job coach, who called Tim. When Tim explained his worries to him, the job coach knew exactly what to do.

"When you give Tim a direction to do something he's never done before, give a demonstration instead of just telling him. Then ask him to show you how to do it," the coach told Tim's boss.

From then on, the boss gave instructions that taught Tim exactly what to do and prevented him from getting anxious. By the way, the boss started giving similar instructions to all of her adolescent help. She learned that this type of directions ensured that all of them "got it."

One other aspect of disclosure involves completing job applications. Families and adolescents are encouraged to consult with their local vocational counselor or job coach regarding ways to address this issue on specific applications. In addition, helpful information is available at the Americans with Disabilities Act (ADA) Web site (www.usdoj.gov/disabilities/htm.)

ADLs

"ADLs" are the activities of daily living. They include self-help skills, domestic and community skills, socialization, and coping tactics. Ironically, even for the exceptionally bright adolescent with AS, ADLs are often a downfall. It's no wonder that the DSM-IV includes "clinically significant impairment in daily role function-ing" in the list of criteria for AS.

There are probably many reasons for this "relative weakness" in ADLs. Self-help skills and domestic and community responsibili-ties are likely to tax the sensory and organizational skills of adoles-cents with AS. Just when that shirt is starting to feel comfortable, he's expected to change it! Or, heaven forbid, wash it himself? Sleeping in the clothes he plans to wear to school tomorrow saves a lot of steps in the morning—"But, Mom, you're always yelling at me to hurry." And tooth brushing and hair combing take a remark-able amount of motor planning. In addition, many adolescents with AS aren't yet concerned about what others think about their appearance. It's also hard for them to take the perspective of the other person who might be offended by body odor. Perhaps, most importantly of all, there are a lot of things in life that are more interesting than ADLs.

Another of the common reasons for relative lack of daily living skills in adolescents with AS is that it's easy for the adults to over-look this part of the child's "program" when so many other things need so much work. This dilemma may be phrased as, "If we have to set up behavior plans to get the homework done and turned in, who has time and energy for nagging about chores?"

Real life, though, requires at least some mastery of ADLs. Unless all of our children are lucky enough to marry a cheerful and com-petent housekeeper/personal assistant, they'll need to know how to do some of this themselves. So, before they finish school and/or leave home, we need to turn the energy of our working partnership to helping adolescents learn to:

○ Choose clothes appropriate for the situation (i.e., no belly shirts or Grateful Dead T's for the job interview)
○ Launder clothing

CHANGING SCHOOLS

Most students will change schools at least once during adolescence. Typically, the change involves moving to a place that is larger, more complex, and more challenging to every domain of functioning. Students with AS face many of the same anxieties as their peers when making these changes. However, their overall sensitivity to change can sometimes make it even more difficult than for their peers, unless we help them with a transition plan. Don't forget—the student must be a working partner with you, if the transition is to be successful.

1. Start planning early—for example in January or February before a September transition. Make a written transition plan that includes points such those listed below.

2. Talk with the adolescent about his or her concerns about the new school. Make a list of questions to research.

3. Start to make a list of the "little" (and not so little) things that make it easier for the student to make it through the day.

4. Several months prior to transition, the "old" and "new" teams should observe the other setting. Look for differences that may challenge the student in the new setting.

5. As a team, list skills that can be addressed in the familiar setting before the student leaves.

6. As a team, list supports that will facilitate transition and adjustment to the new school. Don't forget to include supports such as placement of a friend in some of the student's classes and lunch period. Order any equipment (such as a laptop computer) that the student will need.

7. Make a plan for training staff members who are new to AS.

8. Provide tours of the new school. At least the first tour should occur when school is not in session. Answer the questions that the student has posed. Allow the student to visit as many times as he or she wishes.

9. Help the student say his or her goodbyes at the old school.

10. Prior to the beginning of school, provide another tour. Help the student find his or her locker and practice the combination. Help him or her walk through the daily schedule. Introduce key administrators and professionals (such as the nurse, librarian, and computer specialist).

11. If possible, help the student to make a connection with a faculty member who shares a common interest with the student (or one who sponsors an after-school club that might interest the student).

12. Have a team meeting a few days before classes start, to ensure that everything is all set.

13. Make sure the student has "standing appointments" with the counselor or mentor during the first several weeks of school. Don't wait for him or her to seek help.

14. Have a team meeting three to four weeks into school. Invite someone from the "old" team to provide a perspective.

15. Praise everyone involved for a transition well done!

- ○ Plan nutritious meals and shop for groceries
- ○ Follow recipes for favorite dishes
- ○ Pick up after themselves and do basic housecleaning
- ○ Keep track of important personal papers
- ○ Manage simple banking transactions and follow a budget
- ○ Take care of car upkeep and expenses
- ○ Follow a schedule, including doctor's appointments and social engagements
- ○ Get to work on time, even when tired
- ○ Notify friends, employers, doctors, etc., of changes in plans
- ○ Move safely about the community

EDUCATION

For some, the end of adolescence means the end of formal education. For others, it just means a "change in placement" from high school to college or trade school. For adolescents and young adults without AS, these changes often signal the end of educational and financial support from parents, or, at the least, a change in the expectations regarding support. For adolescents with AS, however, the end of adolescence may not be the right time for this change. In fact, our best guesses suggest that many students with AS are not ready to live independently upon completing their high school years. What can families and adolescents do to ensure that the adolescent receives necessary support to prepare him or her to leave the nest?

IDEA—THE INDIVIDUALS WITH DISABILITIES EDUCATION ACT

IDEA, a federal law most recently revised in 1997, guarantees a "free and appropriate public education in the least restrictive environment" to all students with disabilities. This law applies to students who have a "disabling condition" and are identified as educationally handicapped. Almost everyone knows that eligibility for these services begins at the age of three. Not as many people realize that individuals with disabilities are eligible for these services through the age of 21. Additionally, IDEA mandates that "transition planning" begin at age fourteen and that specific desired outcomes be determined when the student is sixteen. The basic principle is that schools and families are obligated to begin the process well in advance of the end of high school. (The IDEA legislation and a wealth of helpful information are available at www.ideapractices.org).

There are several important aspects of IDEA for high school students with AS. These relate primarily to the transition from school to the "real world" after school.

THE RIGHT TO SELF-DETERMINATION

Under IDEA, adolescents with AS or other disabilities are entitled to be full-fledged members of their educational teams. (This right is further protected under the Rehabilitation Act Amendments of 1998. See www.nationalrehab.org for more information.) Most students require some preparation in order to participate in staffings and IEP meetings. Advanced warning about who will attend, what will be discussed, how long the meeting will last, and what the student might be asked to say usually provides adequate preparation. Regardless of how stressful the initial staffings might be for the adolescent, most students, families, and educators find the process to be the ultimate demonstration of a working partnership.

(By the way, a student's rights under IDEA are transferred to the individual when he or she reaches the age of eighteen, unless the student has been deemed incompetent by the courts.)

EVALUATION AND TRANSITION PLANNING

Transition planning rests upon comprehensive evaluation of the student's strengths, interests, and needs. A critical part of the transition process is the determination of what constitutes a comprehensive assessment. At the very least, the evaluation should include:

○ Formal and informal assessment of cognitive ability (including executive functions) and achievement
○ Formal and informal assessment of communication and social/emotional competence

○ Functional assessment of sensorimotor competence
○ Assessment of interests (through a variety of assessment techniques)
○ Observation of work skills, at school, at home, and on the job (if appropriate)
○ Assessment of adaptive behavior and ADLs, including leisure and self-management skills
○ Consideration of the student's dreams for the future

For many students and their teams, the transition-planning process is aided by participation in a person-centered planning process (such as the MAPS, the McGill Action Planning System).

THE HIGH SCHOOL DIPLOMA

At some point in the transition-planning process, the student, parents, and educational team consider whether the student will receive a diploma or a "certificate of completion." The critical factors in this decision-making process are quite variable, depending upon state law and local district policy. In fact, even as I write this, some states are struggling with the question of whether any student can receive a diploma without passing certain competency examinations.

For many of our more able high-school students with AS, though, the question is not one of whether he or she can qualify for a diploma. The grades and test scores of these students may represent their areas of greatest accomplishment. For these students, the question is more appropriately, "Do we want him or her to receive the diploma on time?" Receiving the diploma effectively removes the student's eligibility for educational services under IDEA and discharges him or her into the "real world" of adult services. (For this reason, a school cannot decide to grant a high-school diploma to a student without written prior notice to the parents and/or student.) For these students, we want to consider very carefully whether our transition goals will really be achieved when the student meets his or her course requirements. If not, postponing the granting of the diploma is a viable option.

SKILLS FOR LIFE

As suggested above, transition planning should not focus simply on whether the student has met course requirements for graduation. IDEA clearly allows the team to consider the need for community experiences, vocational training, and other "life skills" necessary for success in the "real world."

ADA—AMERICANS WITH DISABILITIES ACT OF 1990

Although many adolescents with AS qualify for special education services under IDEA, others present with such strengths that they have not been considered to have an educational handicap. For these students, certain supports are available under the civil rights legislation (ADA). In fact, parents of these children may have used a "504 Plan" under ADA to secure "reasonable accommodations" for their son or daughter.

ADA can be used to support the needs of the student in a variety of educational or occupational settings. For example, ADA provides the backup to request extra time for tests or exams or a quiet setting in which to take a test. For a student with handwriting constraints, ADA supports the need for a laptop computer or voice-activated recorder in class. For a student with auditory sensitivities, ADA can facilitate access to a quiet study room in the library so the student can avoid the long tables in the main hall.

In general, the ADA language and conditions are not as stringent as those of IDEA. As a result, students and families sometimes have to work creatively with the educational setting to determine what constitutes a "reasonable accommodation." For most students, though, the effort clearly pays off in the long run. The specifics of ADA legislation and its growing case law are available at www.usdoj.gov/disabilities.htm.

COLLEGES AND VOCATIONAL SCHOOLS

Although students with AS are usually viewed as bright individuals, there is substantial anecdotal evidence that they are underrepresented in college and vocational school populations. Given that most students with AS compare favorably to their peers on cognitive ability and academic achievement, we must look to other explanations for their difficulties on the college campus.

EXECUTIVE FUNCTIONS AND STAYING ON TOP OF THINGS

Without a doubt, one challenge for the student with Asperger Syndrome revolves around inefficiencies in organization, planning, and self-management. In middle and high school, structure, predictability, parental support, and (often) special education services compensated for the student's relative weaknesses in these executive functions. Very few colleges or vocational schools offer this degree of support. In planning for post-high school education, it's important to do two things: (1) teach organization and self-management every day in every way during high school and (2) seek an educational setting that provides learning centers, tutoring, coaching, and other supports for the student with AS. (*Peterson's Colleges with Programs for Students with Learning Disabilities or Attention Deficit Disorder* provides a helpful, though incomplete, listing of colleges. Other resources are available online.)

MANAGING THE SOCIAL SCENE

Not surprisingly, it's the social aspect of college and vocational school that is most challenging to many students with AS. They may have trouble tolerating the habits of roommates or floor-mates. They often are distressed by the rule violations ("Quiet hours start at ten. What is she doing with her stereo blasting?"). They can be overwhelmed by the sexuality of their peers or by the presence of alcohol and drugs. It's important to teach the advanced version of the "rules of the road" to any college-bound student with AS.

For students with AS who do manage to go away to school, several interventions are quite helpful. First, it does help to have a single room. And if the campus offers "quiet dorms" this can be another help. Soliciting the support of the residence advisor is often beneficial. In addition, many students with AS benefit from a formal or informal "Circle of Friends" (individuals who come together regularly to help the student with particular challenges).

Whenever possible, it's also helpful to set up structured social interactions. For example, I know one young woman who couldn't tolerate the uncertainty of the dining hall. As a result, she was skipping meals and subsisting on foods that could be prepared in her hot pot in her dorm room. Once we put her in touch with with a wheelchair-bound student with great social skills but limited mobility, she felt that she had a role to play.

In general, it is helpful for students with AS to attend smaller colleges or universities that have a school within a school. Within these smaller communities, the adolescent with AS is less likely to fall in the cracks.

JOBS AND CAREERS

Some students with AS are not interested in moving on to college or trade school. A few have discovered a niche that they want to pursue. These students may be self-sufficient in their niche, perhaps with the moral and financial support of family.

Others just don't know what they want to study, and they hesitate to go to school without direction (perhaps unlike some of their non-AS peers!). For the adolescent with AS who does not qualify for public job counseling and training, it's often worthwhile to pursue vocational assessment in the private sector.

ADULT SERVICES

Some students with AS are not ready to go to college or to vocational school because of inadequate skills. For these adolescents and young adults, it is imperative to establish their connections with the appropriate state agency for adult services. These services may be provided by a variety of state agencies, depending upon state bureaucracy and the individual's strengths and challenges. For example, in one New England state, services are provided by the developmental disabilities agencies for students with below average intellectual functioning, and by the mental health centers for individuals with higher levels of cognitive functioning. Check the regulations in your state.

In addition, it is important to establish connections with the local vocational rehabilitation agencies. This may be done under the "umbrella" of other adult services, or it may be separate. (For information regarding an individual's rights to rehabilitation services, visit www.nationalrehab.org.) Vocational services allow access to job counseling, job coaches, and a variety of supported employment opportunities.

If all has gone according to schedule, transition planning will include establishing connections with appropriate adult service agencies. If this has not happened for you or your son or daughter, call the local developmental disabilities or mental health center.

FINANCES AND OTHER MATTERS

Nobody likes to think about money—especially in terms of providing for the financial needs of our offspring, should something happen to us or to them. But careful planning is essential for the parents of children and adolescents with AS, both to ensure that their needs are met and to ensure their access to resources.

ESTATE PLANNING

Even before your child reaches adolescence, it's important to consult an attorney who is well versed in estate planning for families of children with disabilities. (This is important even for families of extremely competent individuals with AS.) As your adolescent moves toward emancipation, his or her needs will become even more apparent. At that juncture, wills and estate planning become absolutely essential (even if you think you don't have enough money to constitute an estate).

HEALTH INSURANCE

Most of us are accustomed to having our children carried on our group health insurance plan. This works fine as long as they are full-time students. Under most plans, though, coverage for dependents ceases when they reach the age of majority (age eighteen) and are no longer full-time students.

Many plans also carry the provision that coverage can continue for dependents who meet certain criteria for a disability. Check with your employer or your insurance plan to determine what you need to provide in terms of documentation.

Additionally, some individuals with AS qualify for health insurance through Medicaid or Medicare. These determinations are not based upon financial need but on the specialized medical needs of the individual. Check with your state Disability Determination Unit for details.

MENTAL HEALTH SERVICES

Some adolescents and young adults with AS require mental health treatment because of anxiety or mood disorders such as depression. Even those who are not anxious or depressed can benefit from mental health services designed to teach social skills, coping, or self-sufficiency. These services may be provided through your local mental health center or through private practitioners. In many states, AS (as one of the autism spectrum/pervasive developmental disorders) is considered a "parity condition." This means that treatment must be covered by health insurance at the same rate as any other medical condition. Check on parity in your state, to ensure that your son or daughter has adequate coverage in the event that mental health services are needed.

MENTORS

Think of the mentors in your life. Maybe a teacher or a coach. Maybe a neighbor or the parent of one of your friends. Maybe a peer. What did that person provide? If you're like many of us, your mentor served as a sounding board and a cheerleader, as a confidant(e) and the objective voice of reality.

Adolescents and young adults with AS need mentors, too. They need mentors to bear witness to their experience of life. To brainstorm about problems. To share successes and to bemoan disappointments.

Mentors listen and listen and listen. They believe in their "mentee"—even when that person doesn't believe in him- or herself. They model problem solving and provide another point of view. Mentors seldom preach, and, if they do, they do it subtly. Some therapists are mentors. Some teachers are mentors. Some parents are mentors. Some friends or siblings are mentors.

In the end, it doesn't matter who is the individual's mentor. But it does help to have one.

Mary Jane came into her therapy session and announced that she needed to make a plan to talk her mother into letting her dye her hair blue. She brought a magazine to illustrate the various methods of turning brown hair blue. She talked eloquently about her reasons for wanting blue hair. She listed the people she had consulted about the wisdom of this undertaking.

Mary Jane's therapist was appalled (at least, in her mind). Why not crimson? Or even bright orange? But blue?! And how could Mary Jane's mother ever agree to this? Wouldn't this brand Mary Jane as even more different, at her conservative high school?

Fortunately, the therapist knew Mary Jane and her family quite well. She knew that the family was skilled at finding compromises between Mary Jane's artistic inclinations and the culture of her family and community. The therapist suggested that Mary Jane might overwhelm her mother with a sudden move from brown to "permanent blue." Weren't there some temporary or less dramatic measures?

Mary Jane and her therapist talked about how to talk with her mother. "Mom, I really want to dye my hair blue, but I know that might be too much for you. Can we talk about a compromise?" The therapist wrote down this opening statement as Mary Jane dictated.

Then Mary Jane decided to write more, in "her own words." As Mary Jane spoke aloud and wrote, she came around to her own "softened" view. "Maybe I can just try some of those hair crayons to see what blue highlights look like."

Mary Jane didn't need someone to tell her what to do. She needed someone to bear witness to her own feelings and thought processes. She needed someone to stand with her as she considered a range of options. She needed someone to respect her while she came to her own conclusions. Adolescents and young adults with AS truly benefit from mentors.

A FINAL NOTE

Parents often ask, "What is the prognosis?" "What will become of my child in adulthood?"

The truth is, we really don't know yet. We haven't had enough time to follow large numbers of individuals with AS as they pass through the developmental stages of adulthood.

What we do know is this. Some individuals with AS continue to gain social awareness and social skills well into adulthood. They learn more and more about the rules of the social road, and they become indistinguishable from other shy or introverted people. They may marry and have children. They often have satisfying careers. Other individuals with AS find a niche, a profession or a vocation that allows them to pursue their passions in solitude and satisfaction. Perhaps they are not the most social among us, but they get by. Some individuals with AS are less fortunate. They remain underemployed or lonely. These individuals are at risk for anxiety or depression.

Who falls into which group? It's too soon to tell for sure. But we do have some hunches, based upon the life journeys of people in general. It helps to have a passion, something that fascinates you and leads you to continue to learn and grow. It helps to remain active and fit. And it helps to remain connected with at least one other human being.

For none of us should be forced to travel life's journey alone.

Postscript

Over the last several months, I have looked forward to the day when this manuscript could go in the mail. Finding time to write seemed like such a challenge. The possibility that I might misrepresent someone's feelings made me nervous. Eagerness to share stories and ideas made me want to hurry through.

But here I am, on the last page, with tears in my eyes. It has been a profoundly touching experience to reflect on all the children and adolescents and families I have known. It has been heartening to remember all of the lessons learned from so many people. I've recalled the wisdom shared by colleagues. I've been humbled by the knowledge and passion and commitment that keep everyone going. And, now, on the last page, I'm having trouble ending!

But, end I must.

Oliver Wendell Holmes once wrote, "A mind that is stretched to a new idea never returns to its original dimension." As you and your "working partners" make your journey down the roads of life, I hope that this book sends you off with minds stretched by new ideas and fueled by renewed passion.

Appendix

Task Card:
  Doing Laundry

Algorithms and Graphic Organizers:
  Concept Map
  Venn Diagram
  Paragraph Template
  Test-taking Algorithm

Social Stories:
  The Middle-School Dance
  Sleeping Over at a Friend's House

Task Card

DOING LAUNDRY

STUFF I NEED:

Dirty clothes
Detergent
Stain stick
Washing machine
Dryer
Drying rack

DON'T

1. Mix whites and colored clothes.
2. Wash colored clothes on "hot" or "warm."
3. Leave wet clothes in the dryer.
4. Forget to fold and put clothes away.

STEPS:

1. Make two piles of clothes: white clothes and colored clothes.
2. Do a load of white clothes first.
3. Choose "Warm/Cold" temperature. Turn the dial to "Wash" and pull it out.
4. Put in 1/4 cup of detergent.
5. Look at each piece of clothing. Apply stain stick on any stains. Put in washer.
6. Fill the washer as full as the top ring on the agitator. Leave extra clothes for another load.
7. If the washer stops, check to see if it finished the cycle. If not, rearrange the clothes and pull the dial out again.
8. If the cycle is finished, take out clothing one piece at a time.
9. Hang underwear on the drying rack. Place everything else in the dryer.
10. Set the dryer for 2 marks past "Less Dry." Push the start button.
11. When the buzzer buzzes, take out the clothes and fold them right away.
12. Put the clothes away.
13. Follow the same steps for colored clothes, except use "Cold/Cold."

Concept Map

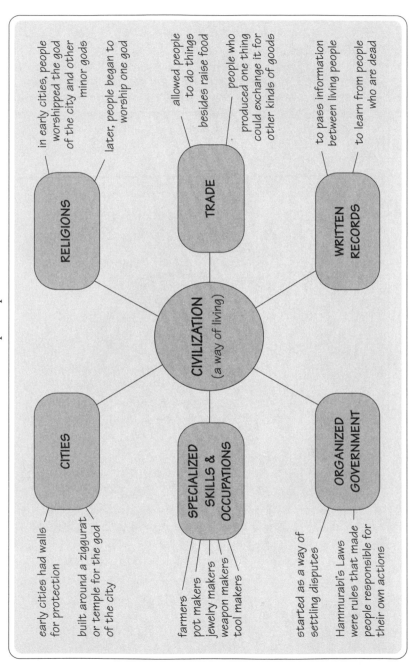

Venn Diagram

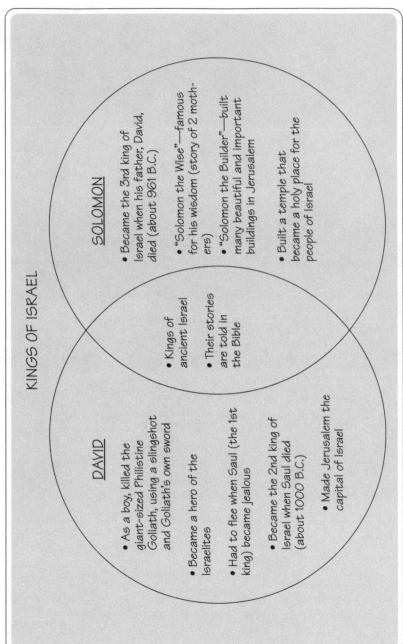

KINGS OF ISRAEL

DAVID

- As a boy, killed the giant-sized Philistine Goliath, using a slingshot and Goliath's own sword
- Became a hero of the Israelites
- Had to flee when Saul (the 1st king) became jealous
- Became the 2nd king of Israel when Saul died (about 1000 B.C.)
- Made Jerusalem the capital of Israel

- Kings of ancient Israel
- Their stories are told in the Bible

SOLOMON

- Became the 3rd king of Israel when his father, David, died (about 961 B.C.)
- "Solomon the Wise"—famous for his wisdom (story of 2 mothers)
- "Solomon the Builder"—built many beautiful and important buildings in Jerusalem
- Built a temple that became a holy place for the people of Israel

Paragraph Template

PERSUASIVE PARAGRAPH

Topic Sentence: Seniors should be able to leave school grounds during lunch.

Detail #1: Not enough cafeteria space

Detail #2: Learn real world skills for spending & saving $

Detail #3: Practice manners

Detail #4: Practice time-management and responsibility

Detail #5: Support local economy

Concluding/Clincher Sentence: As you can see, there are many convincing reasons to let seniors leave school for lunch.

Test-Taking Algorithm

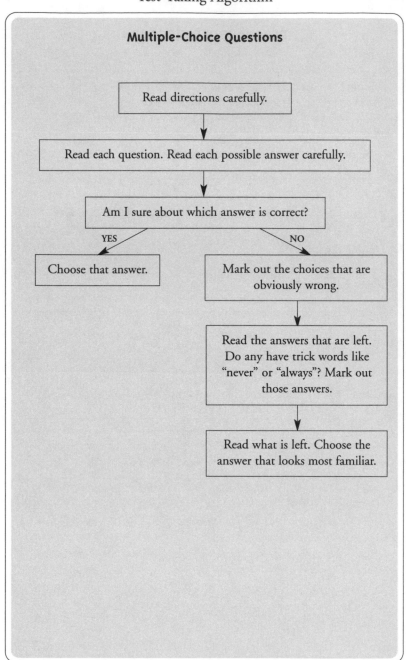

Social Stories

THE MIDDLE SCHOOL DANCE

It's almost time for the middle school dance. Lots of kids go to the dances. Some kids don't. I think I'll go to the next dance.

Most kids go home from school and change clothes before the dance. The guys wear cargo pants, T-shirts, and button-down shirts over them. They don't wear coats and ties. The girls sometimes get dressed up in sparkly tops and black stretch pants. Some girls even wear dresses. Some of the girls even put on makeup.

Dances start at 7 o'clock. Parents drop kids off at school. Some kids ride with their friends, so they don't have to go in alone. When we get to school, we go into the gym. Lots of kids are there. Some adults are there. Some of the adults are teachers or coaches. A few might be parents. But most of our parents go home.

At my school, a disc jockey (called a DJ) plays music on the loud-speakers. The music is pretty loud, but we get used to it. Kids stand around and listen to music. They talk to their friends and laugh, a lot. Some of the guys act kind of silly, but not too silly. They drink sodas from the concession stands.

Sometimes kids dance. At my school, nobody does fast dances. I don't know why, but that's the way it is. When a guy and a girl dance, they slow dance. Sometimes a girl asks a guy to dance. Sometimes a guy asks a girl. Just because a guy and a girl dance doesn't mean they're going out.

About 10 o'clock the dance is over. We say goodbye to our friends. Parents meet us in the parking lot. Then we go home.

Dances make some kids nervous. They get worried about what to talk about. They get worried about dancing. Sometimes they worry that no one will talk with them.

The best way to handle dances is to know what to expect. It also helps to go with a friend. That way there's someone to talk to. It isn't cool to stand with your friend the whole time, but it is good to know that there's somebody to go back to.

Next time my school has a dance, I think I'll go. I'll try to find a friend to go with me. I think I can handle the loud music. I may even ask someone to slow dance!

Social Stories

SLEEPING OVER AT A FRIEND'S HOUSE

Sometimes I get to sleep over at a friend's house. It's fun to spend the night, because then we have more time to do stuff together.

Sometimes I eat dinner with my friend and his family. They usually have food that I like. If I don't like it, I just eat a tiny bit. I don't complain, though. That might hurt their feelings.

Sometimes I go over after dinner. That's okay, too, because my parents know what I don't like to eat.

After dinner, my friend and I usually watch a movie or play video games. My friend asks me what I want to do first, because he's trying to be a good host. It's nice for him to ask. But it's not a good idea for me to be bossy all night long. That might hurt his feelings.

I don't like to sleep on the floor. Neither does my friend. We usually flip for who gets the bed. If I lose the flip, I try not to complain. I try to be a good sport. I can always take a nap tomorrow afternoon.

My friend likes to stay up super late. I usually fall asleep first. That's okay with my friend, because he knows me pretty well by now.

Sometimes I have to go home really early the next morning. If I have to leave early, I try not to complain about missing breakfast. My mom or dad can get me something to eat on the way to wherever we're going.

Sometimes I get to stay around in the morning. Then my friend and I can eat breakfast. Even if I don't like their kind of cereal, I try not to complain. I can always eat something else later.

My friend is usually a good host. I've been practicing being a good guest. And I always try to remember to tell his parents "thank you" when I leave.

Resources

American Psychiatric Association (2000). *Diagnostic and Statistical Manual of Mental Disorders* (4th edition-Text Revision). Washington, D.C. American Psychiatric Association.

Asperger, H. (1991). 'Autistic psychopathy' in childhood. In U. Frith (Ed. And Trans.), *Autism and Asperger Syndrome.* Cambridge: Cambridge University Press. (Original work published 1944)

Attwood, T. (1998). *Asperger's Syndrome: A guide for parents and professionals.* London: Jessica Kingsley Publishers.

Cumine, V., Leach, J., & Stevenson, G. (1998). *Asperger Syndrome: A practical guide for teachers.* London: David Fulton Publishers.

Duke, M.P., Nowicki, S., & Martin, E.A. (1996). *Teaching Your Child the Language of Social Success.* Atlanta: Peachtree Publishers.

Fling, E. (2000). *Eating an Artichoke.* London: Jessica Kingsley Publishers.

Freeman, S., & Dake, L. (1996). *Teach Me Language: A manual for children with Autism, Asperger Syndrome and related developmental disorders.* Langley, British Columbia, Canada: SKF Books.

Fullerton, A., Stratton, J., Coyne, P., & Gray, C. (1996). *Higher Functioning Adolescents and Young Adults with Autism.* Austin, TX: Pro-Ed.

Frith, U. (Ed.)(1991). *Asperger and His Syndrome.* Cambridge: Cambridge University Press. Austin, TX: Pro-Ed.

Gray, C. (1995) *Social Stories Unlimited: Social stories, comic strip conversations, and related instructional techniques.* Jenison, MI: Jenison Public Schools.

Inspiration Software, Inc. www.inspiration.com

Klin, A., Volkmar, F.R., & Sparrow, S.S. (2000). *Asperger Syndrome*. New York: Guilford Press.

LINKS: Strategies across the curriculum. (1998) Woburn, MA: Educational Performance Systems, Inc.

Myles, B.S., & Simpson, R.L. (1998). *Asperger Syndrome: A guide for educators and parents.* Austin, TX: Pro-Ed.

Myles, B.S., & Southwick, J. (1999). *Asperger Syndrome and Difficult Moments: Practical solutions for tantrums, rages, and meltdowns.* Shawnee Mission, KS: Autism Asperger Publishing Co.

Nowicki, S., & Duke, M.P. (1992). *Helping the Child Who Doesn't Fit In.* Atlanta: Peachtree Publishers.

Schopler, E., Mesibov, G.B., & Kunce, L.J. (1998). *Asperger Syndrome or High-functioning Autism?* New York: Plenum Press.

The Source. Quarterly newsletter of the Asperger Syndrome Coalition of the United States. (info@asc-us.org).

Thompson, S. (1997). *The Source for Nonverbal Learning Disorders.* East Moline, IL: LinguiSystems.

Willey, L.H. (1999). *Pretending To Be Normal.* London: Jessica Kingsley Publishers.

Williams, D. (1994). *Somebody Somewhere.* New York: Times Books.

Williams, M.S., & Shellenberger, S. (1996). *How Does Your Engine Run? A Leader's Guide to The Alert Program for Self-regulation.* Albuquerque, NM: TherapyWorks, Inc.